DATE DUE

Communicating with Children

Collected papers

Longman Papers on Residential Work

Children in Care edited by Robert Tod
Disturbed Children edited by Robert Tod
Therapy in Child Care by Barbara Dockar-Drysdale
Consultation in Child Care by Barbara Dockar-Drysdale

Longman Papers on Social Work

Social Work in Adoption edited by Robert Tod
Social Work in Foster Care edited by Robert Tod
Communicating with Children edited by Eileen Holgate

Communicating with Children

Collected papers

Edited by Eileen Holgate

With a foreword by Clare Winnicott, OBE

Longman

LONGMAN GROUP LIMITED
London

Associated companies, branches and representatives throughout the world

© *Longman Group Limited 1972*

First published 1972

ISBN 0582 42833 5

*Set in 11 on 12 point Monotype Garamond,
and printed in Great Britain
by Western Printing Services Ltd, Bristol*

Contents

Contents

Foreword

The writing of a foreword to Eileen Holgate's collection of papers on communicating with children does not in itself seem to be a necessary exercise. To all who have ears to hear the papers speak for themselves and no additional word is needed to reinforce the message, nor could any other voice be expected to penetrate further than the voices of the children themselves.

For me the value of having the opportunity to write a brief foreword is an entirely personal matter in that it gives me the opportunity to identify with those who make the effort, and have the courage, to communicate with children in the kinds of situations in which social workers meet them. No work can be more rewarding in terms of response. The response shows how desperately children need to communicate, and the use made of the opportunity is out of all proportion to the actual time involved. In other words the dividends on the investment in this kind of work are high. As one writer in this collection says: 'I aim to get them to talk about almost anything because, once started, they will reveal with surprising speed something that is important to them' (M. K. McCullough).

In her introduction to these papers Eileen Holgate suggests that there is no answer to the student's question, 'How do you make children talk?' I agree with the comments made, including the recognition that talking and communicating are not the same thing, and that the latter requires all the professional skill that can be mustered, together with a belief in the need to recognize the individuality of each child.

The papers in this volume show that the key factor in this matter of establishing communication is the creation of basic trust between child and adult. The building up of trust is a complex, interactive process, and as Selma Fraiberg points out in her first paper (no. 7), the child's own interviewing techniques in this process are impressive. On the whole the younger the child, the more impressive tends to be his ability to test out and to sum up the adult.

It is possibly true to say that the younger the child, the more hope he is likely to bring to this new relationship. In theory we know that this is a fair assumption, although in practice we know that previous experience can alter the picture for better or for worse at any age.

It seems important that this set of papers, which calls urgent attention to the fact that children need and can use personal help and understanding, should appear at this moment in time. The present tendency away from work with individual clients and towards the attempt to make more effective use of resources in the immediate environment is entirely understandable. Moreover, in terms of current needs and unused resources it is inevitable. At its best this development could add a much needed dimension to social work practice, but whether or not it will do so entirely depends on the quality of the clinical understanding which social workers bring to their task. Such understanding can only be acquired through work with clients as individuals. The depth of human need can never be fully fathomed or met, but only exposure to it and responsibility for it on a person to person basis can give any reliable guidelines as to the help needed, and how it might be given. There are no short cuts to understanding, and in the last analysis everything depends on this ability. By its emphasis on knowing children as individuals and working with them on this basis (whether they are seen singly or in a small group setting), this book will not only increase understanding of individual children in stressful circumstances, but will surely also lead to a more informed use of community resources for the relief of distress.

C. Winnicott

Clare Winnicott, OBE, now Senior Lecturer in Social Work at the London School of Economics, was Director of Child Care Studies at the Central Training Council in Child Care, 1964–71.

Acknowledgements

I would like to acknowledge with thanks permission to reproduce articles in this book from the following journals and authors:

Case Conference, formerly published jointly by the Association of Social Workers and Case Conference Ltd, Ruskin House, Coombe Road, Croydon, CR0 1BD, and Miss J. C. Brown and Mrs R. O. Prestage respectively for nos 4 and 10.

Child Welfare, Child Welfare League of America, Inc., 67 Irving Place, New York, NY 10003, USA, and Mr R. A. Holzhauer and Mr L. Jacobucci respectively for nos 1 and 2.

Children, Children's Bureau, United States Department of Health, Education and Welfare, Washington, DC 20201, USA, and Mr H. A. Richman, Miss J. O'Neill, Mr M. Schreiber and Miss M. Feeley respectively for nos 6, 11 and 12.

New Society, the weekly review of the social sciences, 128 Long Acre, London WC2, and Miss O. Stevenson and Miss M. K. McCullough respectively for nos 9 and 14. *New Society*, August 1963 and February 1963.

Social Casework, Family Service Association of America, 44 East 23rd Street, New York, NY 10010, USA, and Mr D. D. Eikenberry and Mrs Selma Fraiberg respectively for nos 5, 7 and 8.

Social Work, National Association of Social Workers, 2 Park Avenue, New York, NY 10016, USA, and Miss T. C. Jacobs for no. 3.

Ruth McKnight for '*Group Work with Children* by Ruth McKnight.

I also wish to express my gratitude to Mr Robert Tod for his advice and guidance.

E.H.

Introduction

The social work student who asked, 'How do you make children talk?' was voicing the question which many people have posed to themselves when faced with the uncommunicative child. Failure to elicit a response is unnerving and disquieting to the adult, especially the social worker whose professional responsibility is to help children in distress. Whereas a natural reaction to the child in physical pain is to reach out and comfort him, often wordlessly, the same spontaneity is lacking when the pain is concealed. Yet there are vast numbers of children of all ages silently calling out for help. They range widely from the withdrawn, unhappy isolate who shuns adult contact because it has proved too hurtful in the past and who, wrongly perhaps, is deemed incapable of making satisfying relationships, through the temporarily upset and confused child to the charming, lively extrovert whose bright conversation and easy social manner suggest an ability to relate which he may not, in fact, possess. Such children, whether or not they live with their families, are pleading in myriad ways to be noticed, to be heard and understood, even if they indicate by signs and symptoms rather than words the measure of their need.

Whatever the degree of help and support required, it will never be known if the social worker denies the child his right to be a client. How else can diagnosis be made, a treatment plan be formulated if his needs, the strengths of his feelings and his capacity to relate are unknown? Cogent explanations are given for intensive work being done in other areas. For example, contact with the child in residential care is irregular because of the demands made by families with problems. Yet in such families, attention is often focused on the mother, not the child. Incipient difficulties recognized at an early stage through contact with him would be a valuable contribution in the preventive field. Is it possible that failure to work directly with the child may stem from the worker's feeling of inadequacy and bewilderment? Is she sometimes as threatened as he is?

In the belief that methods of communicating with children tried out successfully by others would be of interest to social workers, I began my collection of articles. Comment must, however, be made on the dearth of literature about social work with children; the inevitable conclusion appears to be that it is a neglected area of practice. Fortunately, as the selection in this book reveals, there are social workers in Britain and the United States who feel a very great responsibility towards their child clients. It is not, of course, possible to copy anyone else's technique. A few people are able to respond intuitively and appropriately to a child's needs, but most, men and women alike, have to learn a professional skill. The social worker whose opening gambit with some children was, 'Can you whistle?' was offering his individual way of finding common ground at the beginning of a relationship. He did not immediately inhibit communication by wanting to know why the child was a truant or a thief; questions in any case impossible to answer, but so often asked. They shared a probably untuneful activity and tension was reduced. They were able to laugh together. And with that amount of implicit understanding, a contact was made which could grow.

Division of the articles is not as clearcut as the four sections might indicate, but it seemed useful to place together first those which highlight the intensity and complexity of a child's emotions; then those giving examples of individual children being helped to understand the reality of their situation; followed by those primarily concerned with inner feelings, and finally those about group work with children. Overall, the focus of the book is on communication between child and adult which is an essential element in any form of healing relationship. The articles demonstrate the fact that sometimes apparently simple responses to a child's needs are enabling. In the casework examples, stories, play, car rides, are shared activities illustrating an indirect approach which offers a neutral area for exploration of tender feelings. The child's imagination may be fired by a new activity, like using a tape recorder, or he may enjoy the prestige of prowess in a particular direction. But it is as well to remember that not all children are inarticulate, not all fail to respond to the traditional interview. If the adolescent's expectation is that he will be interviewed in an office with the worker behind a desk, he will be disconcerted by the worker who, on first acquaintance, draws up a chair cosily beside him or suggests going to the local coffee bar in order to break down formalities.

Group work, as described in the articles, is a valuable resource: part of the treatment, not just a current fashion or an attempt to deal with more children in a shorter time because of the heavy demands made on social workers. It gives depth to the picture of the child as he is seen relating both to adults and to his peers. Many of the activities are educational and have the added advantage of widening horizons for the socially deprived. There is also a place in any group for someone who has time to listen to the child with few opportunities to talk at home.

The quality of work with children can only be as good as the worker's appreciation of the task and her correct interpretation of the level of her involvement, whether she is dealing with the child in isolation, the child away from the family but maintaining his links with it, or the child continuing to live with his family. No matter how effective she feels her relationship to be, in a particular case there may be some other person with a closer one which should be recognized and encouraged. Cooperation and coordination are essential components of the treatment plan and they are aptly illustrated in the articles, regardless of the setting. Collectively the social workers reveal in their writing an awareness of whole situations. They keep clearly in their minds that there may be a number of people involved. Their capacity to relate to children is both objective and subjective. Their individual contribution includes warmth, imagination, creativity, a lively involvement in the interests of children at all ages and stages of physical and emotional development. Like most social workers, they reveal themselves as busy people, but they are readily available to the children requiring help. They accept conflicting feelings; stand firm and resolute in the face of extreme provocation; they know that fantasies revealed are less frightening than those bottled up; they prepare the child for new experiences. There is an impression of flexibility in treatment plans. Joan Brown and

Robina Prestage comment with honesty on those 'unworthy' feelings social workers are sometimes thought not to possess – of anger, boredom, frustration. None claims instant success; they speak of continuity, of patiently waiting for signs of change. They respond to the cues, they pick up the nuances, knowing when to delve into the painful areas and when to desist. Their aim is not to protect, not to give false assurances; it is rather to help the child face the reality of his situation; accepting that through the acknowledgement of suffering comes self-knowledge and growth. Great are the demands made on these social workers but equally great is their satisfaction when progress is made. Contact with children in distress is not all grey and gloomy; it is challenging, refreshing, rewarding.

The children in this collection of articles include adolescents who might be outraged at the idea that they are given no separate identification, but those whom the social worker sees often make the same sort of emotional demands as the younger child. They need a relationship with an accepting adult and it may well be the worker on whom they lean most heavily because no one else has proved equal to the task. The adolescent can usually put his feelings into words, so making communication easier, but he needs encouragement towards independence; in some settings he requires help to face the consequences of his behaviour and to relate to the normal demands of living. He may rail against the imposition of limits, that is the prerogative of teenagers, but he may appreciate them as a token of care and concern.

Children respond to their relationship with an individual social worker, particularly where there is a lack of other close ties. In the residential setting which, with the importance now attached to rehabilitation and community care, is increasingly seen as temporary, the worker provides continuity which is essential to wellbeing. The rapid changes of staff in some agencies may have an unfortunate effect on some children, reinforcing their fantasy that they are 'bad' and only worthy of rejection. Social workers in management positions should recognize the value of a continuing contact between worker and child, and support efforts to maintain this regardless of geographical consideration. Carefully conceived regional plans may enable more children, removed from their homes, to remain in their own areas but administrative convenience sometimes precludes, even in these circumstances, the same worker from dealing with the family and the child. Sadly, some social workers are content that it should be so.

Emphasis has been placed so far on the child who has become the focus of social work intervention. The needs of his siblings should not be forgotten and the fact that they respond to opportunities for discussion is borne out by the articles of O'Neill and Schreiber and Feeley in this collection. Remembered, too, should be the needs of children in ordinary families facing a crisis. Perhaps the old adage, 'Children should be seen and not heard', requires amendment to 'Children should be both seen and heard.' Or better still, a new one written and placed in a prominent position in social work agencies, 'Every child has the right to be the focus of someone's special attention.'

There is no answer to the question posed at the beginning of this Introduction. It may be possible to make children talk, but words dragged from a reluctant, defensive child will not lead to meaningful communication. This can only come from a belief in the importance of individualizing the child and offering him direct help derived from the imaginative use of professional understanding, knowledge and skill.

E.H.

I
Children communicating

I
A child's hour

Child Welfare, vol. 37, no. 4, April 1958

Robert A Holzhauer

Although Robert Holzhauer's article might be described as emotive and dramatic, it seems to highlight all the issues of children in distress. Nine-year-old Jackie is rejected, unwanted, unloved. He has a growing belief, reinforced by earlier unhappy experiences, that he is unlovable. The intensity of the pain communicates itself. The overriding question is whether we, the social workers in the situation, have the strengths to respond appropriately to the challenge of such misery. We have met children who behave like this and we reach out to them. For how long? Are we not sometimes guilty of failing to sustain the contact and wanting to hand over to someone else – anyone else – the child whom we label as a failure? Perhaps the label should be pinned on us because we have been too busy; too preoccupied with a hundred and one administrative details to support an apparently unresponsive child through the crisis created by the adult world.

Many scenes come to mind as I think of the children who come to be with me, not just for fun, although they may say that, but because they need to be with a grown-up who will understand that they are almost always in anxiety or turmoil. For those children the hour we are together is like a pool of all the deep, dammed-up feelings and experiences of the past, of the unrecognized present and the future which never goes beyond fantasy. What I write about them in records, what I think professionally, can be said, but sometimes there is more, something spontaneous, which gives more than a tug at the heartstrings. For I am also part of the present, the past and the future of each child.

There is Jackie, for instance. Only yesterday, Jackie knelt in the corner of my office, his blond hair pushed against the wall as I let the silence fill the room. I walked over to him and touched his shoulder. He threw my hand off with a frantic convulsion. 'Get off me,' he said, his voice strained through dry tears. For a moment he turned his tear-streaked face, his feelings glaring with a raw hurt, intense as that from an unseen wound.

What was I to do for Jackie, aged nine? I could not ignore him, but he was not able to bear the cutting kindness of physical closeness. I could only exert my will to be intensely with him in this desperate involvement of love and hate. We were lost in this office, as distant as if lost in limitless space. Nothing was near, but Jackie's fright at the possibility of needing me. We were unable to move away from or toward each other.

I said softly, 'Jackie,' and stopped as his voice grated against my effort, putting up a wall between any gentleness and his fears. 'You hate me. Get out of here. Everybody hates me.' He pushed harder against the wall. 'They'd have to.'

I felt a rise of hope as he said again, firmly, 'They'd have to.' He was beginning to speak of himself against the powerful adult world and at least beginning to admit he had a self, a bad one. Now, although he turned his back to me, he could begin to hear me. Although he pushed me away, not trusting, he could begin to know me, believe that I might understand. He may learn with me where love lies, entwined as it has been for him with hate.

Jackie pushed against the wall, roughing his head on the plaster. The wall of stone and bricks and steel held. This was an unemotional strength, it did not move away or toward him. It was strong and powerful, but not like an angered, towering adult. It was still and supporting. He kept pushing against the wall, away from me, the unknown human. He pressed to the irrefragable wall which was not subject to his will, as I was not. As he pushed harder he found a new hurt; he was less powerful than the wall. His rage burst forth and, unable to control fury at his helplessness, he exploded, fist pounding, cursing until I stopped him firmly, letting him know I did not want him to hurt himself. But he would be in some way, for in every moment Jackie faced the windmills of fantasy, tortuous and bewildering, as he fought reality.

When I left my office I could not leave behind the forces of feelings which had been engaged in this interplay of two people in a dynamic meeting, beyond their social selves, but not completely lost in mystery at the feelings. I walked past the dormitory where Jackie lived with the other boys, all of them either unblessed at birth, or whose good fortune was hard to find, misery hovered so often about them. Jackie had come only a few weeks earlier to live with them. We hoped he had come to know a richer life induced through care and nurture and therapy. We hoped to get to know him. What he had known before this we could not know and he could not truly know, himself.

A mother almost perpetually in rage, a drunken father often abandoning the family, barren rooms, threadbare clothing. His brothers and sisters sprouting up like wild furies. His own anger mounting, his frustrations overwhelming. The circle of increasing destruction, stealing, fighting, until he was finally frantic, out of control, a whirlwind of force in the frightening tumult. In his few years, trauma had suffused Jackie with anger toward all, fear and rage against himself. But with all of this, as he fretfully lay in his bed, wet from his own anger, sucking his thumb, he was keeping himself alive. A primitive relic of undeveloped infancy burned his body.

On my way home I thought about Jackie. He had drowned all of the dolls last week. He was especially angry at the baby dolls. 'Too damn many babies around,' he said with a flash of temper, almost accusing me. It would have been nice for Jackie to feel he was the main one, the only one, or the loved one. Anything, anybody that interfered with what he wanted and needed was too damn much. There had been so little attention and warmth, there was so little to share, and babies always seemed to have their own way. In his bedroom, the first he had to himself, we had found food under the mattress, on the window sills, in his shoes. 'You won't hit me, will you?' he had pleaded, although at first he was angry. There had been little enough love, little food to share and here there was enough for everybody, every day. He wondered when it would suddenly stop, when would we catch on that he was bad.

The next day when I returned to the office, Jackie was sitting on the steps, his face flushed and anxious. His eyes were cold with tension. He glared at me and then burst out, 'Where were you? Will you be here all day? Will you see me again? When is it my time to see you?' He had wondered what had happened to me after he had been so angry. Had his rage hurt me, could I still like him? In the dark of the night had I left him, as he had been so often hurt and left desolate again? When would I turn into the sullen man, the drunken father who disappeared? When would I not be there for Jackie? Separation and return again and again.

Now only nine, Jackie is miserable. And what after this, after our care? I feel he will eventually be able to accept love, but who will take him to give it? When I am talking with him, when I am just with him, how, at the look from his eyes, shifting with a timeless fear, can I be more than silent as I feel awed by the great question his very existence poses. What will he find after the nightmare of his childhood? Will he some day be reached for, asked for by some family who can richly foster a child, whose home will care for and nourish him?

Robert Holzhauer is a graduate of the School of Social Work, Wisconsin University. He attended the Chicago Institute for Psychoanalysis and was enrolled in the Child Therapy Program there. He has been employed in treatment centres for the emotionally disturbed, in correctional institutions, and guidance clinics, at college and community levels. At present he is Assistant Professor at the University of Wisconsin-Milwaukee School of Social Welfare.

2
Nancy's ride

Child Welfare, vol. 37, no. 8, October 1958

Louis Jacobucci

This is a true account of what a little girl said, in words and action, during a one and a half hour trip in the car from her foster home to an adoptive home. It provides an insight into the terrifying maelstrom of emotions experienced by a bewildered child. We sense her desire to become the powerful, controlling, grown-up because it is so wretched being impotent and dependent in a seemingly hostile world. There is a crescendo of sensation, culminating in momentary blind panic, before she allows herself to become the child again cushioned by protecting adults.

Nancy knew everything there was to know in the world. She knew that mummies worked all day and couldn't take care of little girls. Daddies worked nights and took care of them in the daytime. Nancy remembered that she had lived with lots of people called 'aunts' and 'uncles', and it wasn't safe to like these people too much because you had to leave them, or they left you, and then you would ache inside if you liked them.

What Nancy wanted more than anything else in the world was for somebody to love her. But this was such a secret, she did not even dare to think about it. She secretly wanted to be a baby and to be held and cuddled. Then she wouldn't need to pretend to be big any more. But at three and a half Nancy had already learned that it wasn't safe to be a baby because then you are so helpless, and people can do anything they want with you. It was safer to pretend to be a grown-up because then you could tell other people what to do. But Nancy knew it was hard to be grown up all the time, too, because she couldn't always know what was right for her, and sometimes she got so mixed up and frightened with all the things she had to pretend about. Right now she would have to pretend she really didn't care about leaving this auntie and that she wasn't scared of going with Miss French.

Now Nancy was waiting for Miss French and the man to take her to her new mummy and daddy. Auntie had packed her suitcase and she was going to take her toy box and her bicycle, too. This was her own bicycle that her real daddy and mummy bought for her. Why hadn't they visited her any more? Miss French said she was not going to see them again – she was going to live with her new mummy and daddy for always. She didn't like that Miss French – it was all her fault. She took her away from her real parents and brought her here and now she was going to take her away again.

Nancy remembered visiting her new parents yesterday for lunch. They bought her a dolly and a swing and two new dresses and a cot. Nancy didn't think she would sleep in the cot because that was for babies, and Nancy was such a big girl.

Nancy saw the green car coming with Miss French and the man with the funny glasses.

Goodbye, Auntie, I'm going now. Goodbye, silly doggy – barking at Nancy all the time. Don't forget my bicycle, mister, put it in the car and take my toy chest, too. Now take my dolly by the hand, mister. Let my dolly drive – I don't trust you.

Give me your necklace, Miss French, quick, put it on me. Now give me your earrings, too. Now *I* am Miss French and you are Nancy. Now I can tell you what to do. Now I am not helpless. You are a cowboy, Miss French, and I am shooting you. Bang! You're dead. You're dead, too, mister. You are stupid, goopid, poopid, both of you are stupid and I don't like you. I am mad at you. I'll hit you with this necklace – there and there – and I'll hit you, too. I hurt you, good, you stupid things. You're a bad girl, Miss French – bad, bad, and you're a bad boy. I am laughing. My eyes feel like crying but I am laughing.

No, I don't see the bridge, Miss French. Where? No, I don't see it. No, I won't look at it and I won't see anything. No, I don't see the road. I see the signs and I will scream at the signs. They frighten me. They are strange and tell about strange places so I will destroy them. Did you hear that scream? Here comes another sign. Did you hear that scream? And here's another one, and another, and another. I'll scream at all the signs and I'll hurt Miss French's ears and the man's ears, too.

This is the wrong road, mister; this is a funny road. It makes my stomach feel funny. Now my finger is stuck in my mouth. Look Miss French, my finger is stuck in my mouth and I can't get it out. You help me – no, you can't help me – nobody can help me. Now my two hands are stuck in my mouth. I'm in the water and I'm sinking. I can't get out – I'm going under. I'm sinking, I'm sinking. Help me, help me, please, please.

Are you here, Miss French? Why does your voice sound so far away? Did you leave me? I can hear you better now. Yes, I can see you now, Miss French. You're holding me like a baby. You won't let anything happen to me. Is the man here? We are all in the car and we are going to my new mummy and daddy. They bought me this dolly and this hat. Look at the road. I see the bridges and the road now.

Are we almost there? Put on my hat so I look pretty. There's the house with the red tree in front. There's Daddy on the porch. Hello, Daddy, put my bicycle in the garage. Put my suitcase in your car. The suitcase in the attic? I won't need it any more? . . . O.K. Hello, Mummy – take my dresses and let's put them in my room. Yes, this is *my* room, and *my* cot, and *my* dollies, and *my* television set.

Are you going to work, Mummy? Yes, you are, too – Daddy will stay home and you go to work. Oh . . ., Mummy will stay home all the time and care for me?

Here, take back your necklace, Miss French. Oh, I just don't want it any more.

Louis Jacobucci obtained a Master's degree in Social Work in 1952 from Columbia University. At the time the article was written he was employed as a casework supervisor in a Family and Children's Society in New Jersey. For ten years now he has been the Cape Cod District Executive for the Massachusetts Society for the Prevention of Cruelty to Children.

II
Communicating with children about external reality

3
Casework with the very young child in a hospital

Social Work (USA), vol. 3, no. 2, April 1958

Tina Claire Jacobs

Much has been written in Britain about the importance of parental contact with children in hospital and unrestricted visiting is advocated. Whatever the quality of the support given in this way, the social worker still has a vital part to play in helping the child adjust to his separation from home, to prepare him for new procedures and to face with him the reality of his illness and hospitalization. With very young children, the worker has to adapt a technique which seems geared to older, more verbal, clients. That it can be done is illustrated by Miss Jacobs's article detailing her experiences with several preschool children who have suffered prolonged ill-health.

The small child who is ill suffers a disruption of his normal state of wellbeing. When hospitalization becomes necessary, frustrations inevitably occur. An interruption in the child's development may take place with the separation from his parents; it may be necessary for him to make an almost total readjustment. Children often seem to need help in learning to cope with the reality of their illness and hospitalization.

Perhaps the most unique aspect of the Michigan hospital in which I am a social worker is that it is located in a small city yet gives service to a very large geographical area. Many patients come from distant parts of the state and from neighbouring states as well. The children who are treated here often have unusual or chronic or critical illnesses – otherwise they would receive service at a hospital more conveniently located to their homes. Frequently, they must remain for months or return periodically for treatment. Realistic factors, such as distance, may prevent their parents from visiting as often as would be desirable. My responsibility has been primarily centred on the hospitalized children ranging in age from two to fourteen years and with non-communicable diseases. There are approximately sixty such youngsters at a time, with a heavy concentration of children toward the lower end of the age range.

The work has included all the traditional services performed in a teaching hospital setting. There are manifold services to be offered and these vary with each situation but are related in some way to the social and emotional adjustment of the patient and his family. In addition, there are the innumerable ancillary services performed by all personnel associated with the children and which are geared toward making the youngster more comfortable and happy. Our wards are well staffed: doctors, nurses, aides, and recreational and school personnel provide programmes of activity and the ever necessary Tender Loving Care. The children are dressed and up and about whenever possible.

What of my 'client', who most often is a tiny tot? Professional orientation leads me to observe the children from a different focus of attention than the other workers on the ward. Miss Fraiberg reminds us that 'the caseworker in any setting who is doing treatment of children is first of all a caseworker and brings a particular type of training and professional background to this work'.[1] It soon becomes apparent that each of the children has a strong reaction to the separation from home and family and to the pain of treatment. The ward is never without at least several small children who are showing their pain and anger, some in a withdrawn way, others in an aggressive way. Expression and recognition of disturbing feelings tend to reduce discomfort and to lead to more satisfactory adjustment. How then to help a child toward this when his vocabulary is limited and his modes of expression are different from those of the older clients with whom we are taught to work?

Patty was just three years old when she was referred to Social Service. More than half her life had been spent in hospitals because of a chronic, infantile skin condition with urological com-

[1] Jeanette Regensberg and Selma Fraiberg, *Direct casework with children*, New York, Family Service Association of America, 1957, p. 15.

plications. This necessitated a regime of soaks, frequent baths, restraints, an unsatisfactory diet, catheterizations, and other painful procedures. The urologist who referred her suspected that voluntary urinary retention was part of the problem.

Patty was the fifth child of middle-aged parents. In the decade preceding her birth, two siblings had died – a sister sixteen years of age and a brother of four. The family is Roman Catholic, the father a regular worker with a position of responsibility. Mrs O had believed she was in menopause when Patty was conceived. Mrs O was very much upset by her pregnancy and, at the time of Patty's birth, the mother experienced the onset of eczema. The mother's adjustment had been precarious throughout Patty's life with many hysterical symptoms. These culminated in a severe anxiety attack necessitating hospitalization just prior to the beginning of my work with the family. An older brother was married and out of the home; a nineteen-year-old sister was in a position of serious rivalry with Patty. Mr O saw his place in the family as that of the breadwinner and seemed to retreat from the emotional problems as much as possible. The parents visited Patty irregularly with great scenes on the part of the child when her mother left.

Fortunately, Patty's parents live within commuting distance of the hospital so that it has been possible to work regularly with them as well as the youngster. This child's problems were so great that, less than a year ago, both medical staff and parents were tempted to 'give up'. A close working relationship with both and casework treatment of the mother effected many changes which contributed greatly to the youngster's improvement. This paper concentrates on the casework contacts with Patty and omits the other aspects.

Patty was a 'holy terror' on the ward. She would have several severe temper tantrums daily, was completely uncooperative with all procedure, was both unloving and unlovable. She was so violent during any type of test that it became almost impossible to perform. Patty rejected attempts by other personnel to offer affection; she could not get along in a play situation. Each time she was discharged from the hospital, readmission became necessary within two weeks.

In setting up a plan of treatment I felt that the child should be directly included, particularly since the mother–child relationship appeared to be a disturbed one and was likely to remain so for some time. It appeared that Patty was alienating herself from all relationships and I suspected that it would take a great deal of time and effort before this youngster could trust an adult. It seemed that until Patty could do this, she would continue to suffer greatly and, unless an assertive effort was made to interfere with her pattern of functioning, she might well become even more severely damaged emotionally.

I started out by seeing Patty daily. Because she let out a howl at the mere approach of a staff member, I discarded my white coat to look different from the other personnel. Despite this change of wardrobe, Patty was not impressed by my presence for some time. Perhaps twenty interviews were spent in sitting by her bed, my expressing interest in her, in what she was doing, in what was happening to her – and getting almost no response. I explained my presence to Patty by telling her that I was a lady who came to see the children in the hospital to talk to them. I liked her and I wanted to be her friend. Gradually, I put out feelers – indicated that I knew she didn't feel well, was sad. I talked to her about some of the things that went on in the hospital – the injections, special trays, being away from home. Finally, Patty began to respond, to talk about neutral subjects, and a friendship between us gradually developed. As she began to trust me, she showed more interest in the people and things around her. The first worry she brought out spontaneously was 'Is my mummy coming?' When I was able to clarify the visiting plan and make arrangements for her mother to visit regularly three times a week, Patty would ask me over and over the same question as if she could not believe me. She would repeat at length: 'My mummy can't come today but she will come tomorrow.' She was able to accept the explanation and, with gradual encouragement, started to be able to tell me about her mother's having been sick (a hysterical episode which had occurred at home) and other family problems. Patty initially denied negative feelings about her medical treatment, but I scrupulously attempted to prepare her for new procedures and to verbalize appropriate feelings for her. As Patty slowly became able to express herself more appropriately, her hospital adjustment improved remarkably. There were still tantrums and explosions, but these were far less frequent and the little girl began to be able to have relationships with other people.

We continued to have our special time together every day, during which Patty came to my office. I sometimes made suggestions as to things we could talk about such as family members, being sick, being scared, the frequent readmissions, treatments, her behaviour, and, slowly, we talked about all of these and she participated actively. This enabled me to give her encouragement and support and to help her to understand better at least some of what was happening to her. For example: I could recognize with Patty that she didn't like the tube (catheter) and that it hurt and made her angry. The doctor needed to do this to help her get well. Lots of children had to have this tube and none of them liked it. But some of them found out that if they didn't jump around quite so much, the doctor could get the tube in and out more quickly and it really wouldn't hurt as much. Of course it was okay to cry because Patty was scared and everyone understood that. No attempt was made to probe into her feelings and explanations were realistic and simple. As she seemed to accept them, she appeared less terrified.

When Patty was discharged, a regular weekly clinic plan was set up. By this time she could tell me of the high spots in the week's events. Some readmissions were necessary but these have become less and less frequent and now she is doing well.

This little girl is, of course, an emotionally disturbed youngster. There are serious psychogenic components in her illness and important problems in her relationship with her mother. She has been physically and emotionally traumatized repeatedly during the developmental period of her life. Patty needs help of a more intensive nature than we can offer her but, when first referred, she was no fit candidate for a child guidance clinic because of her almost constant hospital admissions. Nor could she be accepted at a child psychiatric treatment centre because her need for nursing and medical care was far too great. After psychiatric evaluation early in our contact, it was decided that the social worker would attempt to stabilize somewhat the situation prior to psychiatric treatment. Now her doctor and I feel she is ready for out-patient psychotherapy and it is possible to prepare her for this. In the interview preceding the first visit to the psychiatric unit, I told

Patty that the next time she came, Dr Q and I wanted her to meet a 'talking doctor'. This doctor just wanted to talk with Patty and she could tell him anything she wanted to. Patty asked for reassurance several times that there would be no painful treatments and, after this was given, I suggested we go together to see the new doctor's office so that she wouldn't feel strange. Patty was interested in all of this and seemed to have understood what I had tried to explain to her.

Patty is probably of above average intelligence. She is a good illustration of how a preschool child can make real strides with casework help that actually is not very different from what might be offered an older patient.

Little Maisie is a familiar figure on our ward; she has spent the better part of a year with us. She has had surgery to reconstruct the oesophagus and has just recently become able to eat by mouth. Maisie's home situation is a deprived one and the emotional and social problems are enormous; we are attempting, of course, to deal with these. But, in the meantime, what of two-year-old Maisie? At the time of her admission, she did not speak a word, never smiled, rocked to and fro no matter where she was, banged her head on the sides of the crib, and was unresponsive to everyone. In short, she presented the classical picture of the autistic child and showed no improvement even as her surroundings became more familiar. There were only a few of us to whom she would respond passively – at least permit us to hold her, or offer her warmth and affection, and to try to give her some of the mothering to which she was entitled. I felt that it would be helpful to Maisie if I could establish a trusting relationship with her. Then I could try to understand and meet at least some of her needs. It was difficult, indeed, to communicate with Maisie by means of words in the early part of our relationship but I decided that, with a child of this age, I would try to create an emotional atmosphere in which she would experience some security and comfort.

It is necessary to 'start where the client is' and this meant that I could expect no more of this little girl at the onset of our relationship than that she trust me to the degree of remaining with me. I took her to my office for a short period each workday where my time was undividedly given to her. At first she would just sit on my lap and look at me solemnly and it was several months before she participated actively. During this time, I tried to interest her and spoke soothingly to her. Slowly, she gave indications of wanting to become more a part of the situation – asked to walk and began to display a little initiative. One day she threw down a doll to have it picked up again and perhaps this was her first attempt at play. Interestingly enough, each step forward in her becoming more outgoing has been carried right over to the other people on the ward and she became able to play with them, too. She began to wander down to my office on her own and I know it is a place of special meaning to her. I have tried to give her extra support following traumatic procedures and have frequently reassured her that she is getting better and will be able to eat like the other children. At times I have given her toys which I felt she needed; as you might guess, the toy dishes and other eating utensils are her favourites.

I have found that my direct association with Maisie has enabled me to interpret her needs and behaviour to the other staff people in a far more meaningful way. This is, I believe, one of our most important functions and I think that, whenever possible, interpretations should be practical rather than theoretical. For example, Maisie was sufficiently nourished by means of her gastrostomy feedings and there was considerable extra bother in providing oral satisfaction until such a time as this could be considered as food intake. However, this little girl became visibly upset when the food trolleys rolled onto the ward – would shake and immediately become grumpy. One day Maisie took my hand, pointed to the trolley and said 'I want some'. With this information in hand, it was simple to make arrangements for her to be given at least ice chips at feeding time or a few clear liquids which would enable her to 'eat' too.

She was encouraged to address several of us who were close to her by our first names after we realized that it was too difficult for her to use full names and she had started to call various people 'mummy'. She accepted this plan without difficulty.

Maisie continues to have good moods alternately with the more withdrawn ones. It is a rare sight now, however, to find her rocking back and forth and the head-banging has ceased entirely.

When she is not feeling up to par now, she asks to be held, will sit on my lap and play with my coat button. From time to time she will look up at me and she is able to indicate when she has had enough of the cuddling and is ready to play or chatter. She talks now and sometimes will tell me long stories, will laugh and tease. It is hard to understand all that she says but she knows that I am interested anyway. I have seen her at approximately the same time early each morning and once, when I was very late, she darted away from the play group and came to my office. I noticed also that she was quite sullen each Monday morning and usually would not come with me until I came back a second time later in the day. She did not seem to understand when I tried to explain to her on Fridays about the interval until I was to see her again, and so I decided to say 'good-bye' to her in my coat before the week-ends. I hoped that she would associate the coat with the fact that I would be away but would be coming back as I had assured her. It had some meaning to her because she would generally become quite angry with me when she saw the coat. Of course, as she became older and more verbal, she learned to count and seemed to understand better that it would be 'two more days'. The nurses reported that she seemed outgoing and happy during the weekends. In connection with this, it should be noted that among the staff the social workers have one of the most stable schedules, there is no rotation and, almost always, they are there five days a week. The exception to this occurred when I became ill and was hospitalized for several days to be followed by time away from work. At the time this happened, Maisie was already responding positively to my efforts with her and she expected me to spend time with her each morning. Because she had been deserted so often by others, I felt she should have some explanation as to why I was away. We decided that the hospital school teacher, whom she trusted, would tell her that I had broken my arm, was sick and couldn't come to see her. Miss B would bring her to see me if she wanted to come. Maisie acquiesced passively to this, came in the arms of the teacher, and cried when she saw me. I told her how happy I was to see her, showed her my arm, and explained that I would come back to the ward to see her as soon as I could. This experiment of bringing the child to see me was undertaken with misgivings and yet I doubted that Maisie would understand why

I was away unless she could see it for herself. The experiment proved successful. Maisie spread the tidings of my broken arm by taking each pediatric employee and visiting parent to my darkened office. She would point to the door and explain 'Arm broke – can't come in.'

It is important to mention the inadvisability of becoming the sole person in the life of a small child. My treatment of Maisie would not be successful if she withdrew each time she was separated from me. My time with her is necessarily limited and has been geared to offering additional warmth and understanding and support. The main purpose was to enable her to experience an emotionally positive relationship so that, hopefully, she could trust some other adults too. This goal has been achieved and little Maisie now has a spontaneity and enthusiasm all her own, a desire to share her joys and her sadnesses rather than to keep them all inside herself. Arrangements were made eventually for Maisie to be placed in a foster home following hospital discharge. At the time of placement, she was physically well. It was not possible for her to meet the social worker from the placement agency until the time of discharge and so I attempted to prepare her for the experience. I talked with her about going 'bye-bye', about going in a car with a nice lady to a new house where there would be a mummy and daddy and some other children to play with. We took excursions around the hospital so she could become accustomed to being in new places and seeing new people. When the time came, Maisie went off with her new social worker as planned, and shortly afterward fell asleep in her lap in the car.

The question remains, is this casework? Part of casework is the putting forth the effort to establish a trusting relationship with the client in order that we may understand him better and help him, when we can, with his problems. My training and experience as a social worker contributed greatly to my understanding of her, concern for her, and interest in her. The tools used in the casework treatment of an older client were applied, in this case, to a young child – in a way that was meaningful to her.

Billy was four when we began to treat him for nephrosis – a disease characterized by marked accumulation of fluid in the body. A child with this illness may be very disfigured and uncomfortable as a result of his puffiness and Billy seemed to be particularly afflicted in this way. Billy spends approximately every third month with us. He is good natured, cheerful, cute – a 'model' patient. His family situation is a strong one but when he is at the hospital, Billy is four hundred miles from home.

Billy is the fourth of six children. The home is rural; the father works regularly as a labourer. The parents' marriage is a strong one and no particular behaviour or emotional problems are evident in family members. Billy's development was normal and this is the only known serious illness in the family. The family lives simply; both parents have an elementary school education. The parents' car is old and cannot withstand the trip to the hospital. The local minister drives Billy's parents down to see him occasionally, but the visits are infrequent.

Billy generally feels quite well when he is at the hospital, is up and about, and familiar with the surroundings and personnel. He enjoys the playroom activities and participates actively. At times he feels very ill indeed, and then he will talk to no one and will not even cry. He seems indifferent to medical treatment, including the usually dreaded bloodwork. Because of his attractive appearance and good nature, Billy receives a great deal of positive attention from everyone and there is no outward evidence of problems.

My frequent ward visits make me a familiar person on the ward and, in general, the children accept me as a friendly person and are not frightened. One of them appropriately nicknamed me the 'worry lady' and I explained my interest to Billy in this way when I first spoke with him in my office. I wondered why he needed to come to the hospital and what it was like being here. Billy knew that it was because he was sick and became puffy; he 'liked' the hospital. He seemed surprised when I asked about his family and, as we came to know one another better, he was able to tell me how much he missed them. The family is a happy one and Billy was trying to hold up his end by being a 'good boy'. Because he had been sick for so long, he had incorporated a social standard based on recognition for conformity; he thought that by being 'good', he would hasten his return home. When Billy is in the hospital, I see him for regular interviews about once a week, and leave the time open for him to bring up any worries and generally check to see how his emotional health is bearing up under the strain of separation from home. Although at first he was not able to express his longing directly, Billy began to appear for a short visit with me at the times that his roommates had company. Gradually, he has become able to bring out some feelings of resentment toward his parents for leaving him and for not visiting more often. This has enabled me to offer recognition, to talk with him about his family, explain why they could not be with him, to comfort him, and to try to lessen the feelings of abandonment. As Dr Josselyn points out: 'The reassurance that "everything will be all right" is what every sick child wants and needs.'[1]

Billy has learned now that it is all right to cry when he is in pain, that this is understood and accepted. He jumped at the opportunity to have a doctor's kit of his own so that he might practise at giving 'treatment' too. Slowly, he has brought out anxiety about himself: 'I want to be a cowboy when I grow up *if* I get better.' Billy wondered if he would ever be well enough to go to school and brought out feelings of discontent at being so disfigured: 'I don't want to look like Santa Claus.' These were handled realistically with direct reassurance and, when he goes through stages of not feeling well, additional support and encouragement are offered.

Slowly, Billy became able to see that his state of wellbeing did not depend on utter conformity to hospital procedures. He became more aggressive and somewhat more demanding but not excessively so. He had several social problems while in the hospital and appropriately brought them to me so that we might work them out together. These included being bullied by another boy and a room change which he did not understand. Each time, a realistic explanation of what had happened and support seemed to help him.

I have continued to see Billy at the time of his semi-monthly clinic visits so that I will remain a consistent figure in his hospital experience. I hope that having someone away from home with whom he can talk about his feelings at what is happening to him will reduce the permanent impact of his frequent hospitalizations. 'We have learned from psychoanalysis that the period of childhood which precedes the establishment of the superego (roughly

[1] Irene M. Josselyn, MD, *Emotional problems of illness*, Chicago, Science Research Associates, 1953, p. 13.

the first five years of life) is an especially rewarding one from the standpoint of prevention and early correction of emotional disorders.'[1] With a child like this, whose emotional problems are far less serious or obvious than those of either Patty or Maisie, the purpose of a professional relationship is primarily preventive.

This paper gives some examples of what has evolved in work with preschool age children in a hospital setting. In each instance, it would have been preferable to have helped the child's parents carry out their roles more effectively; but because of personal or geographical limitations other methods had to be devised. Toys and play were used only in their natural sense – as an aid in establishing a relationship with a youngster. Colleagues have asked me about the techniques, have seen my work as being highly specialized. Yet, upon review, the principles and methods do not seem very different from those used with an adult client. The difference perhaps is in the need to connect with the experiential world of the very small child. The child, as well as the adult, must be met where he is and the child – of course – is at a lower level of experience. With both, the relationship is used as a means of understanding the individual and his problems and helping him to live more comfortably with himself and his environment.

Tina Jacobs received a Master of Social Service degree from Bryn Mawr College, Pennsylvania, in 1951. Her professional career has been primarily in medical and psychiatric settings. At present she is actively engaged in supervising a foster home programme for mentally retarded children and adults sponsored by the state of California.

[1] Selma Fraiberg, 'Counselling for the parents of the very young child', *Social Casework*, vol. 35, no. 2, February 1954, pp. 47–57.

4
Casework with young children in care

Case Conference, vol. 11, no. 9, March 1965

Joan C Brown

Miss Brown demonstrates that direct contact between the social worker and the child is essential, but this account of the way in which a sense of security is restored to a three-year-old boy and his four-year-old sister in the brief time between removal from deeply disturbed parents to eventual placement with foster parents cannot be read without recognizing the social worker's appreciation of the valuable part played by others, in this case the staff of a children's home, in whatever success is achieved. The fact that it is the housemother who accompanies the children on preliminary visits to the foster home shows a confidence between field and residential workers that is sometimes lacking, to the detriment of everyone concerned, not least the children.

No attempt is made to limit parental contact after difficulties are experienced as a result of their aggressive behaviour at the children's home. Instead office visits are arranged and the car journeys provide one sort of opportunity for discussion with the children about their previous experiences. They are able to verbalize some of their fears and the worker is able to clarify the situation simply for them. A car journey may, however, be threatening to the child who has been removed from his own home by car and he may need time to regain his confidence.

In the title I have thought of the word *casework* in a rather wider sense than the usual definition. In dealing with young children the value of the direct interview is more limited than it is with the adult or even the older child and one has to make use of additional tools, in particular by creating the type of environment in which the child can most satisfactorily develop. By this I do not only mean placing the child in what appears to be a suitable environment and by indirect casework (i.e. guidance of foster parents or house parents) promoting the child's better integration. This, of course, is a common and valid method but it is also possible to use and manipulate the child's environment in a more positive way so as to make a direct contribution to the child's development and, in one sense, this can be regarded as part of a casework process with the child.

I should like to describe work done with two small children – Margaret, aged four years, and Peter, aged three years, during a period of transition lasting about seven months, which will I hope illustrate these points.

These children came into care by Court Order for neglect. The father gambled and drank heavily. The mother also drank and was addicted to drugs. Both were deeply disturbed people. The father was aggressive, violent and paranoiac. The mother was neurotically ill and had spent several short periods in mental hospitals, usually discharging herself, or being removed from hospital by her husband before completing her treatment. The parents quarrelled continuously and violently but there was a strong neurotic bond between them, and although the mother deserted for short periods every so often, the likelihood of total separation was remote.

Following the removal of the children, both parents submitted themselves to medical and psychiatric treatment and showed and maintained a very marked improvement. They kept in close touch with the department and pressed assiduously for the return of the children. Finally the children were allowed home on trial and remained for approximately eight months under the closest supervision. The whole eight months were characterized by violent family storms, followed by lulls when real progress seemed to be made. On three occasions it was decided to remove the children but the mere threat was sufficient to produce a cessation of hostilities between the parents. At last the situation deteriorated to such an extent that the children were removed by the worker, Miss Graham, and the area children's officer, Mr Vincent, at the close of a long and violent interview.

The children were placed initially in a small home intended for the temporary care of up to six children. Their condition gave much cause for concern. Physically they had been well cared for and were clean, healthy and well clothed. Emotionally they were completely confused by the father's constant swinging between lavish affection and violent abuse and by their mother's recent withdrawal in addiction to sedative drugs. They had not been physically ill treated but had witnessed or overheard all their parents' quarrels and talked constantly about their 'bad Daddy who kicked Mummy' or 'shouted at Mummy all the time'. One of Peter's favourite games was with a toy telephone which he used to telephone the police to ask them to come and 'stop Daddy hitting Mummy'. Their drawings were full of 'black witches' and their general play wild, uncontrolled and very destructive. At night, both children were restless and suffered from severe nightmares. Margaret in particular would often wake screaming 'stop it, Daddy' and 'don't say my Mummy is a slut'. Both children were intensely fearful of new experiences or strange people. Peter was enuretic by day and night and had frequent temper tantrums. He was the more disturbed of the two, mainly because most of his father's abuse had been rained on his head rather than Margaret's. He had long periods of withdrawal when he became pale and listless and these occurred particularly when he was subjected to any further stress. The same stress would produce wildly extrovert behaviour in Margaret which was more easily handled. Altogether it was patently obvious that a period of stabilization was essential before any permanent placement could be made. It was decided to leave them where they were, and in order to use this period to the best advantage it was planned to make a concentrated attempt to restore their sense of security not only by guiding the housemother in the best way of handling them but also by direct discussion with the children and by controlling their environment in such a way as to produce the maximum results. I shall deal with the last factor first.

The first move was to establish a fixed, though not too rigid, daily routine so that the children quickly learnt exactly what to expect at any hour of the day. Discipline was gentle but firm, accompanied by plenty of open affection. Shouting at or smacking the children was taboo. This, of course, was normal for the home but enforced even when the children were particularly uncontrolled in their behaviour. For the first six weeks, apart from one shopping expedition to buy new clothes, the children did not go beyond the garden of the home. Within this framework they were gradually enabled to become less frightened and to regard the home itself as literally a 'place of safety'. For several months they were allowed to withdraw as much as they wished when visitors were present, and all invitations for tea, day trips and outside visits were firmly refused. As they began to feel safer their behaviour became more controlled and their play less violent. Their language also toned down and they made definite attempts to be socially acceptable by the use of good manners. However, much of the progress made during this period was offset by the stresses created by parental visits. From the moment of removal they put continuous pressure on the department for access to the children and their attitude in the home was hostile and aggressive. It was felt that this 'violent' invasion of the children's main area of security was too destructive to be permitted to continue and it was decided that in future the meetings should take place in the office. This had the double value of removing from the children's notice the inevitable hostility between the parents and the housemother usurping their parental role and was also an opportunity to widen the children's horizon of safety in a controlled manner.

The office was only five minutes by car from the home. The worker invariably brought them herself, remained available in the office throughout the visit and then returned them without delay. If they arrived before the parents they were taken to the worker's own office, where they were allowed to draw. This occupation was familiarly connected with the worker, who had originally introduced it when supervising the children at home to achieve some quiet in which to talk to the parents. During the parents' visit they called out frequently, 'Where are you, Miss Graham?' and occasionally came to make a personal check. When this routine had been thoroughly established over five or more visits, longer time was spent in the office after a visit and they were enticed into the general office where they were allowed to play with (and incidentally break) such interesting toys as the stapler and the punch. Two or three visits later they came into the tea room and had a biscuit and a glass of cordial. Later again when they had been given particularly good toys by their parents they were taken round each of the offices (about half a dozen) to show their toys to the other officers. Each new venture was accompanied by a barrage of anxious questions, 'Why are we going in here?' 'When are you going to take us back?' 'Will that man hurt us?'

'Will that lady take us away?' However, once safely experienced, then it could be repeated without much trouble. At the end of six months they were completely at ease with the whole office unit and regarded all the staff as reliable and trustworthy people. Indeed they became so relaxed that at times they had to be called to order for using the corridor as a slide. The success of this part of the process was illustrated much later when Peter was brought to the office in the worker's absence and left by his foster mother. The worker found him sitting at the typewriter in the general office, obviously feeling completely safe, and received only the most casual of greetings.

The journey to and fro also provided opportunities to try out new things. For the first three visits the children had been driven straight to the office to make the ordeal of entrusting themselves to a car as brief as possible. On the fourth visit there was no parking space outside the office and the worker announced they would have to 'go round the block'. This met with a storm of disapproval which died away in intense relief as the car again rounded the corner near the office. On the next visit the children demanded to be taken round the block as a treat. On subsequent visits more devious routes were taken and odd bits of shopping undertaken. Gradually the car became acceptable as a safe mode of transport not necessarily connected with being 'taken away'.

At this stage (about the fourth month) the children were introduced to a yet wider circle. Initially car trips were taken along with the housemother with others present. Then they visited other homes with their housemother. Finally they ventured out for short visits on their own to the homes of people familiar to them, and this led directly to their introduction to prospective foster parents.

Over the same period there were frequent discussions with the children, during play in the children's home, in the office while awaiting parental visits, and most valuable of all, in the car going to and from the office. The car obviously aroused the most direct memories and therefore the most open discussion from the children. Originally the children had been told by their mother that she was going to hospital and they had to go away for this reason. When on her visits she was palpably not in hospital she explained they had to find a new house and then they would return home.

Neither explanation was directly challenged, but soon it was clear that both Peter and Margaret, who were very perceptive children, were themselves dissatisfied with what they had been told. Almost invariably they themselves opened the discussion with a question, 'Why did you take us away from home?' 'Will we be going back to Mummy and Daddy?' 'How long does it take to get a house?' Margaret one day described as she saw it, the course of visits to her home when she had been there. 'You used to come and see us every week. When Daddy shouted at Mummy and hit her a lot, Mr Vincent used to come with you and talk to Daddy, and then things would be better and you came on your own again. Then one night when Daddy was being very bad to Mummy and shouting all the time, you and Mr Vincent came and took us away. Why did you do that?' This was a very accurate description of the pattern of visits over the eight months the children were at home. Margaret was helped over a period to understand that they were removed not primarily because of family illness or bad housing, though these contributed, but because being at home when 'Daddy was shouting at Mummy' made them frightened and unhappy and this was a bad thing to happen to them. Peter always listened intently to these discussions, interjecting remarks like, 'I have a bad Daddy who is cruel to Mummy. I'll cut his head off', or 'When I'm grown up I'll get a car like this and run over Daddy when he shouts.' However, for quite a while he confused the issue by asking frequently, usually in a bright tone of voice, 'Am I going home to Mummy today?' 'Is our new house ready yet?' This puzzled everybody as he had had far more unhappy experiences at home than Margaret. Finally it came to light that he was in fact asking about the thing that was most worrying him, rather in the manner of a child who eats the thing he most dislikes first to get it out of the way and like them ran the danger of being given a second helping by mistake. This came to light after a piece of most uncaseworkerlike behaviour. Whenever the worker visited the home, which was very frequently, Peter would immediately say 'Have you come to take me to the office? Will you take me later on? Will you take me tomorrow? Will you take me soon?' etc. Originally this was dealt with in a calm, gentle explanatory way. One day, tired and irritable, the worker said, 'Peter, for heaven's sake stop being such a little pest. I am *not* taking you to the office today, tomorrow or any time this week, so be quiet.' This had the effect of producing a sigh of utter relief, a seraphic smile and the comment 'Good. Now if you will give me a pencil I will draw you a nice picture.' This revelation helped the worker to understand Peter's mental processes more and thus to help him also to understand the situation more fully.

Towards the end of their period in the children's home, both Peter and Margaret began calling the housemother Mummy. This was gently discouraged. 'I'm not Mummy, I'm Auntie Jean, aren't I? You see Mummy at the office.' Later still they began addressing the worker in the car as Mummy. Margaret would then add, 'Aren't I silly, I called you Mummy?' to which the worker would reply, 'Yes, aren't you, because I'm Miss Graham and we've just been to see Mummy at the office.' Peter would sit trying out the names, 'Auntie Jean, Mummy, Miss Graham, Mummy', under his breath. It was obvious that they were aware of the impermanence of their present placement and were looking for something more settled. They were aware of fostering as a fact, partly because Margaret had been boarded out happily while previously in care and partly because, in the interim, many other children had passed through the home and had gone out for day visits, boarding out weekends, etc. At first the children had said defensively, 'We aren't going away, are we?' but later had begun to ask when they would be going for holidays.

After the children had been in the home for about five months and showed so many indications of increasing security and stability, a suitable foster home of all the right qualities was fortunately located. The introductory period lasted for about two months, comprising several visits by the foster parents to the children's home, visits by the children to the foster home, first with their housemother, then without. Weekend visits then followed and finally a holiday followed by permanent placement. The children weathered the move remarkably well, and while their new-found security inevitably received a blow, it was by no means a total setback and the majority of the progress was maintained. After almost twelve months in the foster home there is real hope that the children have a permanent home.

Clearly handling this type of problem in this particular way was helped by a number of physical factors, for example the proximity of the children's home to the office, the size of the home available, the fact that one worker was able to maintain frequent contact throughout. The main point, however, is that what could have been regarded as a mere waiting time between two placements was utilized to the full to restore the children's sense of security and to enable the development of their personalities to go forward in a healthy way.

Joan Brown began her social work career in 1950 as a residential worker in a children's reception centre in Lancashire. She became a child care officer in Essex and later a senior caseworker in Oxford. In 1962 she went to Australia where she was employed as a social worker in the Tasmanian State Social Welfare Department until 1972 when she was appointed Secretary General to the Australian Council of Social Service.

5
A story for Mary

Social Casework, vol. 50, no. 4, April 1969

Dennis D Eikenberry

Knowing that a child is not free to establish satisfying substitute relationships while crippled by the half-understood facts and the pervading fantasies regarding himself and the family from which he has been removed, Dennis Eikenberry seizes the opportunity presented to him by Mary's acknowledged interest in books. He suggests they write her own story and, using this device, he composes an account of her background, taking care to emphasize the strengths as well as the limitations of her parents. In discussing the content of the book, Mary is helped for the first time to express some of her feelings about the past, and eventually is able to make a better adjustment to foster care. Fuller accounts of some of their meetings, together with comments about her reactions to the material, would have been useful.

Besides being such a creative activity, this seems an excellent way of reconstructing a child's previous history, thereby enabling him to develop his own identity. Instead of the illustrations being pictures cut from magazines, it might be possible with other children to use actual family photographs.

It is disheartening to note that relatively little was known about the individual children in Mary's family prior to removing them from home because the parents had been the focus of casework attention. Mary might not have been so confused and upset if she had been prepared for subsequent events.

A major task of a child welfare worker in a protective services agency is to help the children under his care integrate unhappy life experiences and free their potential for establishing satisfying relationships that will ensure their further development. When deprivation and inconsistent parental care lead to a child's separation from his parents, it is essential that the child should understand what is happening to him and why. This article discusses a specific activity that became the medium through which information was conveyed to a young child – preparing a written and illustrated account of the child's past and current life.

Mary's parents, who were Sioux Indians, had been continuously involved in marital conflict. Despite the efforts of social workers for many years to provide rehabilitative services to the family, there was a pattern of frequent separations and abandonment of the children by one or both parents. Court action resulted in awarding custody of the two eldest children to a state training school. Mary's mother placed the four younger children in boarding schools but kept Mary with her until Mary was five years of age, at which time she and her younger brother were removed on a court order charging dependency and neglect. Because the behaviour of the parents had been the primary focus of the workers' helping efforts, they knew relatively little about the individual children prior to their placements. When Mary was placed in a foster home, it was explained to the foster parents that the caseworker needed to get to know Mary and planned to see her regularly outside the home as well as observe her within the foster family setting.

During the first weeks of foster care it was evident that Mary did not know why she was in the foster home. She could not discuss her feelings with the worker, but she revealed fantasies that her mother would buy a house and a car and then take all her children home to live together as a family. Since it was most unlikely that her mother could improve her level of functioning sufficiently to enable her to resume responsibility for the care of her children, Mary's fantasy could not be encouraged.[1] Rather, she needed to be prepared for continued foster care. Mary's ability to cope with her situation indicated that she could use help in understanding and accepting what had happened to her that created the need for a substitute family.[2] Although the worker used play therapy on occasion to convey ideas to Mary, it was the child's interest in the book department of the local store that led

[1] Sidney L. Werkman, 'The psychiatric diagnostic interview with children', *American Journal of Orthopsychiatry*, vol. 35, July 1965, 764–71.

[2] Franklin H. Goldberg, Stanley R. Lesser, and Rena Schulman, 'A conceptual approach and guide to formulating goals in child guidance treatment', *American Journal of Orthopsychiatry*, vol. 36, January 1966, 125–33.

the worker to consider using the preparation of a 'book' as a means of interpretation. On one of their subsequent trips to the store Mary was again attracted to the children's book section and asked the social worker to buy her a book. The social worker responded by offering an alternative – that he and Mary write their own book. Mary was interested in this suggestion and ready to talk about it. The discussion led to a consideration of how to make a book and what materials would be required.

The worker's next trip with Mary was used to select the materials needed. Mary carried primary responsibility for determining what supplies were to be purchased and she appeared to enjoy shopping for them. In response to her question about what the book would be about, the social worker suggested that it be a book about Mary herself. A considerable amount of time was devoted to planning the book. It was agreed that before the next visit the social worker would write the story and Mary would find pictures that would illustrate the story. She selected pictures from magazines and was assisted with her project by the foster parents.

When the worker and Mary met again the story had been written and Mary had a packet of pictures. Together they read the story and selected pictures to illustrate it. The story was typed on large sheets of paper, with a paragraph or two on each page, allowing much room for pictures. The process of putting the book together provided many opportunities to read all or selected parts of the story. Mary determined to a large extent which parts needed to be reread and discussed. As a result, she talked about parts of her life that she had been unable to discuss earlier with the worker. The following is the narrative in the book.

THE STORY OF MARY

In the beautiful land of Chief Red Cloud lived a man named John and a woman named Susan. Red Cloud was one of the early chiefs of the mighty Sioux Nation. Red Cloud's people were some of the first people to live on the great prairies. They hunted wild animals to eat. The berries and other fruits that grew on the prairies and in the Black Hills were good to eat.

John and Susan were some of Red Cloud's people. They were happy that long ago he had been their chief. Sometimes John and

Susan lived in Red Cloud's land. This land is called the Pine Ridge Reservation. Sometimes they lived in a city with a lot of different kinds of people in it. This city is called Rapid City. John and Susan grew some fine babies. Taking care of the babies and finding enough food for them was a hard job. Sometimes it was easier for them to take care of their children and get food for them if John would live in the city and Susan would live on the reservation. Sometimes John and Susan loved each other very much. Sometimes they did not love each other.

When John and Susan had six little children, Susan felt something happy and wonderful inside her and knew she was going to have another baby. Susan took her little children back to the land of Chief Red Cloud. There on the reservation she gave birth to a baby girl. Her name was Mary. She was a pretty baby with beautiful black hair and sparkling eyes.

When Mary was old enough to crawl and stand up alone, her Daddy John was hurt badly in a car accident. He could never walk again. He could not get food for his family and he could not care for them. There had not been many jobs in the city or on the reservation. How sad he was after all this had happened.

By the time Mary could walk well, Mama Susan was ready to have another baby. Now Mary had a little brother. His eyes sparkled too.

As the children grew bigger and stronger they needed more food to keep on growing. They needed someone to help them learn about new things. They needed someone to keep them from getting hurt. Mama Susan had to do all this by herself. Even though she loved her children, it was hard to care for all of them alone.

In the city there were many helpers. Some of these helpers were doctors, some were teachers, and some of the helpers were social workers. The social workers wanted to help Mama Susan so that she could do the things she wanted to do for the children to help them grow big and happy. Sometimes some of the children had to go away to school or live with someone else. Even when there were helpers and when some of the children were somewhere else, it was hard for Mama Susan to do what she wanted to do for her children.

John and Susan talked to some of the social workers about what to do to help the children. They decided that the children would get the best kind of care if they could live with other people. Because by this time John was very sick. It was because John and Susan loved their children that they decided to make these plans for them.

The only way the social workers could put Mary and her little brother in another home was to go to court. In court the judge could say it would be okay to find new homes. If the judge would say this, it would mean that John and Susan would be able to let the children go to new homes.

Susan, Mary, and her little brother and the social workers were in court on two days. They were hard days. Susan cried and said she had wanted to be able to help the children. She was sorry that she had not been able to take care of her children, and she also said she loved them. Mary was unhappy and did not know if she should sit by Susan or sit by the social workers. The judge agreed that the best way to help Mary was to let her live with another family. Then she could have all the things that Mama Susan wanted for her. It was not easy for Mary to tell Mama Susan good-bye because she loved Mama Susan. Mama Susan was a good person to love.

Mr Eikenberry was Mary's social worker. They did not know each other very well before they went to court. It was hard for Mary to know whether Mr Eikenberry could help her and be her friend. Mr Eikenberry knows many children and many families. One of the families he knows are Mum and Dad Thomas.

Mum and Dad Thomas have loved and cared for many children. They had asked Mr Eikenberry for another child to love and care for. Mr Eikenberry talked to them about Mary. They decided that they wanted to take care of Mary as long as she needs their home. Because Mary needed a home and the Thomases needed another little girl, Mr Eikenberry brought Mary to live with the Thomas family.

At first, living with the Thomases was a little hard for Mary. They did some things differently from the way Mary did them. Sometimes Mary would be terribly lonely for the people she had known before.

The Thomases will be Mary's mum and dad for as long as she needs them. They make a good home. Dad Thomas works in the day so he can have food for his family. Mum Thomas spends her days washing clothes, baking cakes and caring for her children. Working and washing and baking are some of the ways the Thomases show that they love their children.

Mum and Dad Thomas have a pretty little yellow house with a white fence around it. The fence keeps the children from going into the street. Some of the children need to live with the Thomases a long time. Some of the children need to live with the Thomases a short time.

The Thomas family is like an Easter basket. Some of the children have white skin. Some have brown skin. Some of them, like Mary, are Red Cloud's people and have a nice tan skin. Some of the children are big, others are just tiny. A few are boys and a few are girls.

All of them like sweets and raisins. They all need to be loved and cared for. They all pray and they all sleep. Sometimes they cry and sometimes they giggle. Not many of them like to go to the doctor for an injection. They all like to feel the rain on their pretty faces. Like Mary, they all need the Thomases for part of the time they are growing up.

EVALUATION OF THE TREATMENT DEVICE

One approach to evaluating this method of handling with a child potentially explosive information about his life is to consider both the potential benefits to him and the difficulties it may create. In regard to Mary it seemed that the book had served much of its intended purpose by the time it was assembled. The process of planning the book, matching the pictures to the narrative, and repeated discussions of the content occupied weekly contacts for two months. Mary was then ready to take the book home and give it to the foster mother for safekeeping. Mary chose to store the book on top of the refrigerator in the kitchen, where it was beyond the reach of the other children in the home. Significance might be attached to her choice because much of the family's activities took place in the large kitchen of the foster home.

Mary's attitude toward the book was one of quiet respect. After her book was completed, her attitude toward her early life appeared to be one of acceptance.[1] The new level of adjustment was effective to the point that it allowed Mary to move beyond expending all her energies in trying to deal with her feelings about the past.

The foster parents were involved in discussions about the book, and they indicated respect for it and its meaning to Mary. They knew enough about Mary's background so that they could talk comfortably about the book with her and handle any questions she might raise.

The social worker consciously attempted to write a story that would be an accurate representation of Mary's natural parents and their situation, referring to their strengths as parents as well as their limitations. By discussing the story in segments with the child, the worker had an opportunity to expand on the contents. Talks about the story as the book was prepared were lengthy and included many details of Mary's background. The guideline in these discussions was to determine what the child was asking for and what she was able to use constructively. The theoretical construct on which the social worker was operating was that Mary's having a clearer understanding of why her own parents could not care for her would make it possible for Mary to effect a more satisfying adjustment to substitute parents.[2] The relationship that developed between Mary and the worker during the preparation of the book enabled him, in the months that followed, to help her face new situations as they occurred, especially conflicts with other children and the death of her father.

One danger in a social worker's writing the story of a child's life is that he may inadvertently emphasize his wish to help the child at the expense of giving an accurate account of his actual life experiences. Safeguards that could be taken to diminish this possibility include the use of colleagues, or consultation, for more objective evaluations as the story is being developed. Accurate representation and interpretation must be a constant concern of the worker.

Another caution relates to a child's readiness and capacity to integrate the information about his life. There should be a definite

[1] Alfred Kadushin, 'Reversibility of trauma: a follow-up study of children adopted when older', *Social Work*, vol. 12, October 1967, 22–33.

[2] Richard H. Seiden, 'Salutary effects of maternal separation', *Social Work*, vol. 10, October 1965, 25–9.

indication that the child wants and can participate in such an experience.[1]

Mary's immediate response to the experience of writing the book and her later adjustment in foster care tends to indicate that this treatment device may have potential value for other children in similar situations. Writing a book about a child's life experiences makes them graphic and tangible for the child and the worker. The book can be used to present therapeutic material of a sophisticated nature on a level that is meaningful and real to a very young child. In Mary's case, the worker learned that two years later the book was still kept on top of the refrigerator. For Mary, who had few mementoes of childhood, the book seemed to serve the purpose of being a part of a developing identity.

Following social work training at the University of Minnesota, Dennis Eikenberry worked in the field of Child Welfare. For five years he was attached to the René Spitz Children's Division of the Fort Logan Mental Health Centre. Currently he is employed as a psychotherapist by the Adams County Mental Health Centre, Colorado. As well as treating individuals of all ages, he has a particular interest in developing techniques for working with entire family units. He is also involved in teaching social workers, probation officers and school teachers.

[1] Grace Ganter and Norman A. Polansky, 'Predicting a child's accessibility to individual treatment from diagnostic groups', *Social Work*, vol. 9, July 1964, 56–63.

6
Casework with a child following heart surgery

Children, vol. 11, no. 5, September/October 1964

Harold A Richman

Within the time limit imposed by a short period of hospital treatment, effective help is given to an eight-year-old boy. Sharing with the social worker imaginative activities including an exclusive club with only two members, finger painting and tape-recorded stories, this frightened child is offered the special relationship he needs with an adult.

A carefully formulated after-care plan enables him to adjust at home to life restricted somewhat by his physical condition. In an active peer group, he is given his own special place with compensating interests. Eventually, as the social worker withdraws, a volunteer from the local community provides a male model which the boy lacks in his fatherless home. He also provides continuing support at a personal rather than professional level.

In a room on the cardiac surgical service of a large research hospital, an eight-year-old boy was engaged in a physical and emotional struggle for life. His name was Tim and he was afraid. As Tim's social worker, I was concerned with his fear, a fear that remained even beyond the immediate physical crisis. As his health slowly began to return, I tried to help this weakened boy wrestle with his fears and nightmares.

The emotional needs of young children during hospitalization are usually met through the security and understanding of the parent–child relationship. Therefore, casework efforts are usually concentrated on helping parents handle their feelings and attitudes so they can be most helpful to their child. Occasionally, however, parents become so overwhelmed or have such a distorted relationship with their child that they are unable to sustain him and direct casework with the child becomes necessary. Such was the case with Tim.

His home broken by his mother's divorce from a psychotic father, Tim lived with two younger siblings and a narcissistic, masochistic mother, herself the product of a disturbed home and ineffectual parents. She appeared to court crisis and disorganization in the family and in her own life and to reject Tim. During Tim's most critical days his mother was demanding and unsupportive, and Tim reacted by withdrawal and depression. Failure of attempts to help her with her relationship with her son, and the extent of Tim's critical emotional needs, made me decide to work directly with him.

Tim was suspicious of strangers. Many new consulting doctors had been seeing him to control post-operative complications; their visits often signalled new and frightening treatments. When I introduced myself as a social worker who wanted to talk to him, Tim said he had just had another heart operation and did not like all the needles he was getting. For several days we talked about his treatments and his family and played some games. On the fourth day I suggested that we form a club to meet, talk, and play together regularly. Tim said he would like that. When I asked him what we should name the club, he answered, 'The Two Men Club' – a tangible expression of his need and readiness for a special relationship. I soon turned my office into our clubroom and, whenever possible, wheeled Tim from the ward to our room.

I hoped to achieve several purposes: to learn how the hospital experience was affecting Tim so I could help him master it, for now and the future; to be a patient, understanding person unconnected with his treatments and medicine, to whom he could talk about his daily ups and downs and thus to help him to accept and benefit from his difficult medical regimen. The club would be a place where he could assert his independence, make decisions rather than simply obey them, talk about new things, have new experiences, and be encouraged, within the hospital limitations, to exercise a boy's natural curiosity. Finally, I hoped our relationship would provide Tim with confidence to express his feelings and give him the experience of having a healthy male relationship.

During our first few meetings, we made clay club badges for ourselves and signs and decorations for the clubroom. Tim participated eagerly as far as his meagre energy allowed. However, he was protective of his thoughts and feelings and quickly changed the subject any time I mentioned his illness. I began to tell stories about an imaginary Robby Robin who fell from his nest. When I asked Tim what happened then, he said that Robby's mother called the doctor. I asked whether Robby was hurt and had to go to the hospital. Tim became tense and said emphatically, 'No,' Robby was not hurt at all. Several days later I asked if we should tell a story about a boy instead of a robin, and he replied softly, but firmly, 'Not about me.'

I did not want to push Tim. We played games, finger painted, and visited the gift shop, the patients' library, and the room with the experimental animals. He responded eagerly to these new experiences, but in his creative play, his art work, and his relationship with me (except for constant complaints about injections) he was restrained and rejected any reference to his own thoughts or experiences. In our play with a doctor's kit, he refused to find anything wrong with the doll patient and would not give injections or medication.

During the second week, while we were finger painting, Tim said very quietly that he could not fall asleep the night before. (The nurses had told me Tim was sleeping fitfully and had a troubled expression on his face while asleep.) When I asked him why, he looked away for a moment and then said easily that he was worried about his roommate who had had a seizure several days before. We had discussed this frightening experience before in a special club meeting I had called the night it happened, so I did not think this was Tim's real worry. But I did not press him.

Over the next week our relationship deepened. We talked more about his troubled sleep and the 'worries' that kept him awake, but he could not get himself to tell me what was worrying him. We made two evening trips to the roof to view a newly launched weather satellite. I gave Tim a picture postcard I brought back after a two-day absence. He kept it inside his shirt. He continued to reach out for new experiences and became more relaxed and spontaneous in our club play.

A turning-point came at the beginning of our third week as Tim pointedly tested our relationship. I mentioned the possibility that he might go home in two weeks. He did not respond to this. Instead, he told me that several other patients had asked to join our club. I told him that this was the 'Two Men Club' and that our

membership was full. I repeated what I had told him many times:
I was his social worker and the club was for us to talk and do
things together. He seemed relieved, then asked what would
happen to the club when he went home. I told him that I might be
able to visit him there. He seemed very pleased and said, 'Maybe
we can find a cabin or a little home where the "Two Men Club"
can meet all alone.' During this period he checked my where-
abouts constantly. I recognized his need to test me before he
could go further with our relationship, so I responded to his demands as much as I could.

On the following day we began ten days of club meetings very
different from those of the previous three weeks. The emphasis
turned from play to talk, a switch Tim himself initiated. During
the previous three weeks we had used the dictaphone in my
office, talking into it and playing it back. Occasionally, I told a
story on it. Tim was a little hesitant to record his voice, but he enjoyed the playback. His recordings usually told what he had done
the day before. On this day I asked Tim if he wanted to tell a story
on a record. Since we had visited the animal room, I suggested it
be about an animal. He told the following story:

> Once upon a time there was a little mouse who did not have
> nobody to play with and nobody to love him. One day he went
> out for a walk into the far, far forest. A lot of animals were
> crying for help because the big elephant was chasing them. The
> little, little mouse grabbed the big, big elephant's tail and swung
> it around his head and threw him out of the jungle. He was the
> bravest mouse in the whole world, and he grew up to be a
> guinea-pig.

As we played the story back, Tim looked frightened and held
his ears. When I told him we did not have to play it back, he insisted that he wanted to hear it. This was the first glimpse Tim had
allowed me of the world in which he was struggling.

There followed three successive club meetings devoted to
stories, all told at Tim's suggestion and all heard back with covered
ears and frightened expression. They told of a world of fear, impotence, violence, and helplessness. These were the stories of the
two succeeding days:

Once upon a time there was a little baby elephant named Panda. He took a walk in the forest where he came upon a big, big deer, and he said 'Hello' to the deer, and the deer said, 'Why, hello,' and they were pals. They walked through the forest until they came to this beaver, and the beaver said, 'You have a spear. I want a spear, but how do I get one?' 'Here's one,' cried the little beaver, so they started out for another walk, and they saw this hunter, and he had a gun, and he was going to shoot them. So they ran back and locked their doors and lived happily ever after.

Once upon a time there was a big dinosaur who thought he was going to die, and he said to himself, 'I am going to die, I know it, I'm going to die.' He walked through the forest and all the other animals were happy but he was the only one who was sad because he was sick.

On the following day we played back some of the old records. The last one told about Robby Robin falling out of his nest. Tim hastened to say that nothing at all had happened to Robby and that he needed neither doctor nor hospital. At this point I had to terminate the meeting and left Tim alone at his request to make a record on his own. This is the record:

Today when Tim and Mr Richman had a meeting of the club, he could not stay long, so we made a couple of records and we listened to them, and after that he went home, I mean where he was going to go. He did not have much time so he got the record player and let me make a record while he was gone. So I did. I made a record and listened to it and I had so much fun that I could not bear to tell this and it was: Once upon a time there was this little robin named Robby Robin, and he set out in the far, far forest, and Robby did not like the animals. One day this great, great big hunter came and he was hunting a whole lot of birds and he killed Robby.

While I recognized the great significance of these stories for Tim, I chose not to discuss them with him. He was getting along well in the ward and club, and I saw the stories not as alarms but as Tim's own way of working out his anxiety about his illness and surgery, within the safe context of our relationship.

Several days later Tim indicated that he needed more direct help. Important visitors were at the hospital and Tim's surgeon was going to speak to them about new advances in heart surgery. Five post-operative children were brought to the sun balcony to meet the visitors before the surgeon's talk. I saw Tim about an hour after the visitors left and he appeared rather dejected. When I asked how the morning had gone, he replied 'OK', but he had not been allowed to hear the surgeon's talk. When I asked about his interest in the talk, he became very tense, said he did not want to talk any more, and mumbled something about 'what he used'. Later that afternoon I saw Tim on the unit and he asked me where I was going after work. He had never done this before, but he would not tell me why he wanted to know. I gave him my telephone number and told him he could call me if he needed me.

The next day I suggested that we talk about the operation. He was reluctant, but I pressed him a little, telling him that I thought I could help him. Then I asked several direct questions: Had he been scared of the operation? Did it still frighten him? Was he worried about it? To each question he answered in a small voice, 'Yes', and began to look frightened. Tears began to roll down his cheeks, but he was not sobbing, and he looked at me as though he wanted me to go on. I said I knew it was hard for him to think about it, but that if we talked about it a little more he might feel better. Then I asked if he could tell me what it was about the operation that he found so scary. The tears continued and he struggled for several minutes before he could whisper, 'The knife.' This admission brought on real crying for several minutes. When he was calmer I asked Tim to describe the knife. He drew, hesitantly, a picture of a large curved knife with a sharp toothed edge.

When I asked how long he thought it was, he held his hands about two feet apart. When I asked what about the knife worried him, he replied, 'What they do with it.' I asked when he thought about it, and he said, 'All the time.' When was it the worst? He said, 'At night, when I dream about it.' Still crying quietly, he told me about the dream that came every night: A huge figure chasing him, wielding an enormous knife. Did other things frighten him? Tim looked at the floor and asked if the blood clots he coughed up were pieces of his heart.

As he used up his meagre energy crying out some of his fears, Tim came close to me and held my arm. I held him for a few minutes, told him I knew that his fears were real and painful, and reassured him about the size of the knife (really only four inches) and the coughing. I could not reassure him that he would not have to undergo the knife again; instead, I emphasized his great progress over the last three weeks. No words or gestures, however, could really soothe the starkness of his terror. I hoped that my presence and our mutual trust would lighten the burden of his fears.

During the next days the nurse reported that Tim's sleeping seemed less disturbed, and three days later Tim told me he had not had the knife nightmare. Later he reported that the nightmare recurred the night before he left the hospital. Three days after our interview about the knife, the doctors decided that Tim could go home the following week and report weekly to our outpatient clinic. He would, however, have to remain quiet and be watched closely.

Tim was reluctant even to talk about going home, so I began the following story. At certain points I stopped and asked him to take over.

Worker: Once upon a time there was a frog. His name was Fog, Fog the Frog. And Fog the Frog lived in a bog. And Fog the Frog who lived in a bog liked to sit in the mud, and he croaked in the mud. He went: Glug, glug, glug. And one day the people from the hospital saw Fog the Frog in the bog and they said: 'We think we should take Fog the Frog out of the bog and bring him to the hospital.' So they asked Fog the Frog whether he would leave the bog and come with them. He said –
Tim: 'Yes.'
Worker: So they took Fog the Frog out of the bog and brought him to the hospital –
Tim: and the hospital took science research on him, just any kind of research –
Worker: and he sat in his little glass house on the seventh floor in the animal room and he went glug, glug, glug. And he thought about where he was, and this is what he thought.
Tim: He didn't like it in the animal room very much –

Worker: and the little mouse who was his nextdoor neighbour said to the frog, 'Why don't you like it at the hospital here in the animal room?' And the frog said –
Tim: 'I don't have any water.'
Worker: Fog the Frog belongs in the bog. But he stayed here for a while, and finally there came a time when he just decided that it was time to go back to the bog, but he didn't know if he wanted to go back to the bog or not because –
Tim: his friend, the mouse, was his nextdoor neighbour –
Worker: and they liked each other, and he couldn't decide whether to go home to the bog or to stay at the hospital. And he thought and thought and he decided –
Tim: to stay at the hospital with his friend the little mouse.

In view of Tim's ambivalence about going home and his investment in our relationship, I decided to continue seeing him during the transition period. Tim's mother had first asked for this plan and she cooperated fully. The time factor and hospital policy dictated that this arrangement could be only temporary. We agreed on a maximum of twelve months.

I visited Tim the day after he went home and then at biweekly intervals for two weeks and weekly thereafter. His physical condition continued to improve and with TV and toys he was keeping himself amused. Our interviews centred on his daily activities and did not deal with any new issues. Since Tim was a child who responded eagerly to new experiences and opportunities, I sought community resources which could help him lead as active a life as he could physically handle. At the same time I was paving the way toward ending my own work with him.

The first priority for Tim was school. He was already a year behind, and for future social as well as academic reasons I was anxious that he should not fall further behind. A local teacher began concentrated instruction at his home. A warm, cheerful woman, her thrice-weekly visits provided a new, engaging relationship for him. In addition, an occupational therapist from the county tuberculosis and heart association visited Tim once a week, leaving craft projects and new games which delighted him. He was soon busy making little gifts for everyone he could think of, including a carefully stitched leather key case for me.

Tim's physical condition improved rapidly. With the early spring weather he was soon outside making friends with the neighbours and playing in the yard. Since he would probably be well enough to go to school in the autumn, I thought it would be helpful for him to have a group experience with normal children beforehand. After a long search, I finally found an excellent day camp for healthy children which would accept him. Located on the grounds of a private school, the camp emphasized crafts, nature study, and sports. Our doctors endorsed Tim's attendance, and the camp director was carefully informed of the boy's limitations and special needs. Our faith in Tim's emotional stability and ability to adjust was wholly vindicated at camp. He fitted into the group beautifully and achieved poise and satisfaction. Visiting one afternoon at Tim's invitation, I saw him try to keep up with his friends in a swimming race. He got tired and a little blue, pulled himself out of the pool, and obviously unhappy, slowly dried himself in a far corner. After a while he came over to me with a smile and led me to the arts and crafts shop to show off the waste-basket he had made for me.

School began, and I visited Tim at home twice in the first month. He was in the second grade and doing well. He got along well with his classmates, but during the first three months he had to be helped to limit his outdoor activity to his physical capabilities. Therefore, I visited the school to talk with the principal about Tim's physical condition. Tim knew about my visit and was pleased.

As Tim associated more with healthy children, it became apparent that he felt more and more pressed to keep up with their activities. Eight-year-old boys place a high premium on activity and Tim was not able to keep up. For his own self-confidence and social development he needed to find some areas in which he could achieve and excel. I arranged for him to join a small Cub troop, where he could develop his interest in scouting skills and nature lore. He responded enthusiastically and gradually became less frustrated at his limitations in the schoolyard.

Ten months after Tim had left the hospital, he and I agreed, both reluctantly, that we would not get together except when he came for a clinic visit. At this time, I arranged with the Big Brothers of America to provide him with a Big Brother. The Big

Brother selected was a family man with a farm outside the city and a strong interest in nature study and outdoor life – an excellent person to provide Tim with the male companionship, identification, and understanding that he now needed so much more on the personal than the professional level.

Three months after my last visit to Tim's house he came into the clinic. His heart was still not well, but he had lost some of the pasty look of a chronically ill child. As we finished a game of darts in my office, he bent over the dictaphone and asked if he could make a record. I was surprised because I thought that our records held bad memories for him. I gave him a blank disc. He hesitated, then asked if he could tell a story alone. I told him I would wait outside. Five minutes later he opened the door and beckoned, then began to play the record he had just made. From the dictaphone came a clear, confident voice – not the hesitant, frightened voice of a year ago.

> I have a friend who is Mr Richman. This is a story about him. Once I had a friend named Mr Richman. He was a good friend. One day I was going to the store and I met him. I had a bag of popcorn and it was all falling out, so he helped me, and we got home fine. Then when we got home, he ate lunch with us, and then he went home.
> The end.

Then Tim picked out an old record at random and played part of it. When he came to the description of the mouse who was so frightened, he smiled and said, 'That was me.' Impressed with the contrast between Tim on this day and the day he left the hospital, I asked him if he remembered our story about Fog the Frog. When he said he did, I reminded him that we never really knew what happened to Fog, and suggested that we finish the story just for fun.

> *Worker*: This is the second story about Fog the Frog, who used to live in the bog. Fog came out of the bog when the people from the hospital came and brought him here, and he stayed here for a while in the animal room until it was time for him to go back to the bog. So Fog the Frog went back to the bog and now we want to find out what happened when he got back to the bog.

Tim: When Fog the Frog got back to the bog he went on his lily pad. Since he wasn't near his lily pad, it was all soaked up because of the rain, but Fog the Frog who lived in the bog got out a new one. It was a brand-new one.

Worker: And he sat on his lily pad and he went glug, glug, glug, which in frog language means –

Tim: thank you and all the people at the hospital for helping me.

Worker: And the people at the hospital said they never had a nicer frog than Fog who came from the bog.

The extent to which I could help Tim depended on our developing a relationship of trust. His naming of the 'Two Men Club' indicated the possibility of his readiness to use a close male relationship. Because such a relationship was new to him, many sessions studded with long awkward silences were required to nurture it. During these sessions play proved to be invaluable as a way to establish rapport.

Considering his background and the intensity of his feelings, Tim's hesitancy to reveal himself was understandable. Even within the safety of an increasingly trusting relationship, Tim found it difficult to express his most troubled feelings – of impotence, helplessness, and fear. In his fantasy world of animals and the jungle he found a medium for expressing them symbolically. However, he feared too much to risk expressing these feelings directly to me, even in fantasy language. Here, the dictaphone played the pivotal role; it could not reject him. That the stories he told were really meant for me was unmistakable from Tim's own behaviour in insisting that I play the records back and then covering his ears in fright. Only after the fantasy had been woven and spoken through the impersonal dictaphone and had been heard, understood, and not rebuffed by me could Tim begin to express his fears directly, as he did about the nightmare and the knife.

I chose an indirect approach in handling the material presented in Tim's stories. I allowed him to tell them without interruption. After carefully listening to the playback, I would make a quiet, general comment about the central theme (fear, death, helplessness) without tying it to Tim or his situation. I always followed this comment with a direct reassurance to Tim that he was doing well and getting better, thus responding to the underlying feelings of doubt and uncertainty which he was expressing through the stories. I chose this approach rather than direct interpretation for several reasons. The mere process of making and listening to the records and having me there seemed to decrease some of Tim's general anxiety. He was becoming more relaxed with me and his behaviour on the unit and during sleep was less agitated. Also, I had the feeling as he watched me listening to the playback that he felt I understood what he was trying to say. In addition, the content of the stories seemed to progress in intensity and closeness to reality, indicating that Tim was moving on his own toward a more direct expression of his feelings. Had Tim appeared more disturbed with me, at play or when asleep, I would have considered either stopping the recording or beginning some direct interpretation, using the story material as a bridge to discussion of his real anxieties. This course would have required consultation and guidance from the psychiatrist and would have required enough time on my part and enough energy on Tim's to deal with the uncovering of deep anxieties.

One of the difficult decisions associated with our relationship was my continuing to see Tim after he left the hospital. Ordinarily, discharged patients who need continued service are referred to an appropriate community agency. Tim's discharge, however, came rather abruptly and at the time of his most intense relationship with me. A break then would have meant a rejection of his hard-won ability to use help. More time was needed to prepare Tim for the termination of our contacts and for the gradual encouragement of his ability to develop other relationships with people in the community who could help him. While our final separation was difficult, it came only after Tim had integrated much of his experience with me, and after the integration had been tested and proved in his use of the community resources provided for him.

The foregoing points describe the conduct and rationale of the work, but they do not touch the heart of the treatment. This was the elemental process of responding to a weakened, struggling child's need for love, strength, and understanding. Tim's sobering words and fears deepened my respect for the impact of critical illness and surgery on children. His growth during the period of our relationship heightened my appreciation of the potential of direct, limited-focus casework treatment in helping sick children.

Tim's future is uncertain. His heart is too damaged to carry him very far and soon he will face another life-threatening operation. I am hopeful that he will be able to approach this experience with increased emotional strength and capacity.

Harold Richman, now Dean and Associate Professor, University of Chicago School of Social Administration, moved from social work into the field of social policy and academic administration. He is Consultant to the United States Senate Subcommittee on Employment, Manpower and Poverty as well as to the Office of the Secretary of Health, Education and Welfare.

III
Communicating with children about inner feelings

7
Some aspects of casework with children
1. Understanding the child client

Social Casework, vol. 33, no. 9, November 1952

Selma Fraiberg

In the first of her two papers, Mrs Selma Fraiberg writes with disarming simplicity about the crucial initial encounter between the social worker and the child client. Not for her the face to face interview at this stage. She understands too well the child's anxieties in a new situation and the threat presented by the direct approach. She understands his need to evaluate the worker while he himself is being evaluated. Carefully planned informality aimed at gaining his confidence, emboldens seven-year-old Jimmy to test the worker's reactions in certain key areas important to little boys, as he throws out his leading questions to her while exploring various parts of the room. Grown-ups have not been very sympathetic towards him in the past, but, judging from her answers, this adult is different, she understands children so he can relax and the interview can proceed.

There is a certain type of client who creates special problems in the administration of social agencies and in the interviewing situation. This client seems totally unable to comprehend the function of a social agency. He frequently creates disorder and chaos in the waiting-room. Often he talks loudly and shrilly, demanding numerous attentions, and has been known to look boldly over the shoulder of a typist as she transcribes confidential reports. In the initial interview with the caseworker, this client states more or less positively that he has no problem and he does not know why he has come to the agency. Further difficulties are encountered when it appears that he cannot sit in a chair for more than five

minutes. He tends to concentrate on irrelevant matters like the operation of the Venetian blinds, the counting of squares on the asphalt
tile floors, the manipulation of paper clips into abstract forms.

The client has neither marital problems nor employment problems. He is not in need of relief, although he will gladly take a
hand-out. The sex of the client may be male or female. The age is
roughly five to fifteen years. What shall we do with him?

The most disconcerting feature of the child client is his inability to behave like a client. He does not come to us because of
his recognition of a need for services or counselling. Someone
else – parent, teacher, physician, the court – has made him the
reluctant consumer of our services. We are embarrassed by such a
client. The body of our techniques is geared to the initial coming
together of a willing and needful client and a willing and resource-
ful social worker. The client who has no recognition of a problem
or who, having one, refuses to talk about it, is known as an 'uncooperative client'.

When we deal with the child client, our concepts of service and
responsibility are turned about, for, willing or not, he becomes
our client, our problem child. Frequently he, like the adult client,
comes to us at a time of crisis in his life. Usually he has not come
to us for direct treatment or psychotherapy; he may not even be
in need of such treatment. Although a few children may be taken
on for direct treatment by the agencies working in the field of
family service, child welfare, school social work, juvenile court
work, or group work, most child clients come to these agencies
either for evaluation and social study or for practical planning and
guidance around critical life problems. It is this group, the major
category of cases referred to social agencies, with which this discussion is mainly concerned.

What do we mean by 'help'? Ronnie is five. His father has deserted the family and the mother has arranged to place him in a
foster home. The social worker, the lady who helps children,
arrives on the scene. She will help him to find a nice home, she
says, where people are very fond of little boys. But does this seem
like 'help' to a child? How helpful is the lady who takes a little
boy away from his mother? We know how it seems to little
children: 'Mother has not sent me away. The lady has taken me
away from mother.'

Or it is another crisis. Peter is eight, and is threatened with expulsion from school after a long series of classroom incidents. He is 'sent' to see the school social worker for diagnostic study. 'This is a man who will help you', he is told. Everyone wants to help Peter. Papa wants to help him and that's why papa beats him with his belt when he is bad. The teachers want to help him, too, and that's why they have to tell him so many things for his own good and why they have to bawl him out even when they don't like to. And now look – here's another person who is going to 'help' Peter. How will he help? Will he recommend that papa give Peter a good spanking? Will he bawl him out for his own good? Will he send him to another school? Or to the remand home?

I recall a little girl of six whom I saw some years ago and who received my offer of 'help' with rather more open-mindedness than is usual with children. She was being seen for study and observation because of her fears regarding death. She seemed grateful to know of the existence of a strange animal like myself and, being a child of today, she was not really surprised that a creature known as a social worker had recently come upon this planet with a mysterious ray or a substance X for distressed children. But within a few visits I noticed a considerable loss in my prestige. My client became bored with my toys (hers were better anyway, she assured me) and sceptical of my methods. One day the client, squirming uncomfortably on a chair, twisted herself around until her head touched the floor. Then, balancing herself nicely, she stood on her head. At this moment, the client, legs in air but beautifully poised, was struck by a thought. She said to the worker, 'You said you knew how to help children when they're afraid.' 'Yes,' said the worker, leaning over to catch the first shy confessions. 'Well, then,' said the client sharply, 'why don't you do it?'

If we ask ourselves why in the world this idea occurred to my client while she was standing on her head, we can only conclude that for her my proposed 'help' was a kind of feat or trick, something I kept up my sleeve, in the same way that she kept her acrobatics on tap for display on special occasions. 'Here, now I've shown you my tricks; you show me yours!'

Like the concept of 'help', the concept of 'worker–client relationship' requires a certain amount of reworking when we consider the child client. Sometimes, with uneasy acknowledgment of the differences in the relationship to adult and child clients, we feel that it is necessary to go under an assumed name for the benefit of the child. In this way a social worker may refer to himself not as a 'caseworker' but as a 'friend'. Unfortunately this avowal of friendship may be received cynically by the child. To a scared youngster this offer of friendship is no more a guarantee of things to come than the famous overture of the Wolf to Little Red Riding Hood, or the invitation of the Spider to the Fly. Actually the word 'caseworker' is a nice empty package for the child who meets one for the first time, and we are in a position to fill it and give it significance by what we do and by what we are to the child.

With all these things in mind, we can see that there are very practical obstacles in the way of gaining a child's confidence and bringing him into a meaningful relationship with someone called a caseworker. If we grant that this relationship is the most important first objective with the child, we shall find ourselves behaving in unorthodox ways to achieve it.

We begin, of course, by putting aside formal interview procedure. We shall see the child, particularly the young child, in a room which is inviting to children but which can be equipped at modest cost. There will be paper and crayons and Plasticine, a few dolls or puppets, some toy cars for the little boys, perhaps a small fire engine. A doll's house and other such equipment can be used but are not necessary. The space under my desk has served at various times as a house, a garage, a fire station, a prison, a burial place for treasure, a secret hideout for robbers, and a refuge for a sulking client. It is practical and economical. Dart games, guns, and other such weapons are found to be quite unnecessary, and besides they are hard on the caseworker. The aggressive urges in children rarely require these accessories. It is also noticeable that nowadays every little boy comes equipped with a built-in sound track for machine-guns and bazookas; there is no need to strain the agency budget for lethal weapons that are only a poor imitation of a little boy imitating a lethal weapon. The cost of equipping such a playroom is very reasonable and any equipment beyond this is an indulgence for the caseworker. Here I speak from my own experience, for I suffer temptations in toy stores like everybody else and I have no difficulty in persuading myself that a certain doll is just what I need for a certain four-year-old who has been getting along just fine without it.

Perhaps this is as good a time as any to raise the question of the use of play as well as play materials in the social agency. Many of the fancy toys and play materials that fill our agency reception rooms and playrooms have dubious value in our work with children. I feel that this applies to child guidance centres as well as agencies that do not specialize in the treatment of children. Experienced child therapists find that such lavish displays of toys are a distraction to the child and do not serve the imagination nearly so well as the spontaneous, invented games of children which can be achieved through a minimum of props and toys. We must all admit, however, that they do serve a purpose for the worker. If we are uncertain about the nature of work with children – if we are troubled by the thought, 'Now whatever shall I do with this child?' – the richness of our playroom equipment can allay our own anxiety.

In the past, too, I have seen how the special 'therapy' toys – the amputation dolls, the ingenious little toilets, the weapons for bringing out aggression – have been defended on the basis that they 'bring out material'. This emphasis on 'getting material' is well worth our attention. We shall dwell on the subject at other points in this discussion, but I should like to raise certain questions at this point. If the amputation doll brings forth from our little five-year-old the expression of a castration anxiety, what do we know of him that is not true of every other little boy of his age? How does this enlarge our diagnostic picture? We cannot even consider this important *unless* the ego of this child has failed to deal satisfactorily with this anxiety; that is, if the ego has been compelled to develop pathological defence mechanisms or symptoms to ward off the anxiety. In other words, our criteria for diagnostic study are obtained not from observation of id-manifestations, but from observations of the ego and its efforts to deal with the instincts. For this we do not need the amputation dolls (which would in any event give a normal child the willies), and we do not need the little toilets. We need very little more than our educated eyes and ears.

But to return to this child whom we've just brought into the caseworker's office. Having put aside the formal across-the-desk interview, we now find ourselves on a completely uncharted course. We introduce ourselves to the child. We size him up – as he does us – and we wonder, 'What *shall* we say to him?'

There are several gambits we can follow, all of which in my own experience lead into blind alleys. If we ask him whether he knows why he has come to see us, he will most certainly say 'no'. If we ask him to guess, he will probably say, 'I don't know'. If we ask him even in the friendliest way if he doesn't have lots of questions he'd like to ask us about why he is here and who we are, he will still, most probably, say 'no'. We can easily guess the trouble. Children hate being questioned. Furthermore, not one of these questions can be answered honestly until our youngster knows just what sort of person we are. If we give him time he will find out what he wants to know about us. And *his* interviewing technique, while devious and oblique, is remarkable in many ways. This junior interviewer can find out more about us in fifteen or twenty minutes than we can find out about him in the same amount of time. Let's see how he does it.

Jimmy is seven. He is referred for diagnostic study and planning by his school. He is reluctant to go to school; he is unable to learn to read although he has average intelligence. The caseworker, after introducing herself, invites him into her office and suggests he have a look around if he likes. He gingerly fingers the toys, picks up a crayon, looks as if he would like to scribble on a piece of paper, then changes his mind. He examines the drawings of other children which hang on the wall. 'Who drew those lousy pictures?' he wants to know. This is a complex question. He doesn't really care 'who' drew the lousy pictures since he doesn't know anyone who comes here. He wants to know the attitude of the caseworker toward such productions. He ridicules these other drawings as if anticipating ridicule from the caseworker for the drawing he might make which might be 'lousy'. The caseworker says: 'Oh, we all draw here when we feel like it. We don't care if we draw good or bad. We don't have to be artists. We just draw for fun. This isn't school, you know.'

He picks up a toy fire engine on which one of the parts is broken. 'Jeez,' he says with some effort at indignation, 'who broke your fire engine?' Now this is really a very good question to test the reactions of adults under stress. Clearly this junior psychologist is not interested in 'who' broke the fire engine, but in what happened to the guy who broke the fire engine. What does the caseworker do? Understanding this question (variations of this question are very common in first interviews with children), the caseworker says, 'Oh, one of the kids broke it, accidentally, but I didn't get mad.' Following this point neatly Jimmy says, 'If he did it on purpose would you get mad?' 'I wouldn't like it, but I don't get mad at children.'

Jimmy brings out a school medical card. 'I like all my teachers in school except Miss Chase. She hits kids sometimes.' The caseworker frowns with disapproval. Jimmy gives her five points on that one.

'You've got a lot of drawers in that desk. What do you need all those drawers for?' The caseworker says, 'Well, let's look and see.' She opens all the drawers so that he can peek inside, finally opens one that is filled with odds and ends of junk, a supply especially maintained for youngsters. There are paper clips, stickers of various kinds, a broken automatic pencil, a pencil sharpener, a cigar box filled with the parts of a broken alarm clock, some marbles, chewing gum, a bar of chocolate. He rummages happily, receives sweets, a stick of gum, and the broken propelling pencil as a souvenir. He is sure he can fix it, he says.

Emboldened by this friendly opening of private drawers on the part of the caseworker, Jimmy now asks, 'Do you have children? How old are you? Are you married?' The caseworker answers these questions simply but truthfully.

Now sticky with sweets and at his ease in this surprising place, Jimmy ventures another question. 'Do you have lots of kids who come here?' he asks. 'Oh, yes.' And then he says pointedly, 'What do the other kids come here for?' The caseworker answers this by giving a few examples – a youngster who used to come here because he got mad too easily and got into lots of fights, a little girl who was afraid of things at night – 'Oh, they come here for lots of reasons.' Then the caseworker asks her question: 'Now tell me,' she says, 'why do you think you come here, Jimmy?' Jimmy looks embarrassed, then mumbles, ' 'Cause I don't like to go to school.'

Admittedly this is a circuitous route to this most vital of questions in a first interview, but its advantages are obvious. The client has had plenty of time to interview the caseworker. We are impressed by his interviewing technique. In a relatively short space of time he has learned the following things about the caseworker. 'She is not like a school teacher; this is not like school. You don't have to do things perfectly here.' (This was obtained from the remarks about the drawings.) 'She does not get mad at children.' (Found out via the fire engine.) 'She doesn't like kids to be spanked.' (Derived from remarks about Miss Chase.) 'It's all right to be curious here.' (Information acquired through comments on drawers and invitation to look.) 'You can ask her any question you want and she'll answer it.' (Established through direct questions regarding worker's age, and so on.)

Now from the client's point of view this is highly pertinent information. If his difficulties lie with school and teachers and school welfare officers, the caseworker needs to be assessed in terms of enemy strength. Attitudes toward behaviour, destructive urges, and the curiosity of little boys must all be inventoried ahead of time. Why tell this lady *anything* about the troubles in school if these revelations are to lead to a lecture, a bawling out, or threats? Since Jimmy has found that adults generally fall into the category of lecturers, scolders, and threateners, he reveals shrewdness and intelligence in first interviewing the caseworker around these vital points.

From the caseworker's point of view, too, we will not deny that a few important facts were gleaned from Jimmy's interview of her. His derogation of the other children's drawings is a possible clue to his own learning disability, a fear of not succeeding, a disparagement of his own products, a feeling that what he can achieve is so unworthy that it isn't worth trying. His fear of punishment from the adult is hinted at twice in his early remarks, and there is the possibility that the fear of adults may enter into his reluctance to go to school. On the positive side is the fact that when he feels safe with this adult he easily surrenders his wariness, and the caseworker knows that this reveals that his fear of authority figures is not all-pervading or frozen; it is manageable and yields to reality testing.

We may be disappointed in these meagre findings. We do not know the symbolic significance of the interest in the broken fire engine or the curiosity about desk drawers. It might be argued that the worker could easily pursue these points. It seems to me that just here is where we so frequently get bogged down in child casework. For if the reaction to the broken fire engine has a deeper significance, we shall surely not learn of it in this first hour and the knowledge would do us very little good anyway. If this were a therapeutic situation, if we had behind us months of work, we might learn about its meaning – or we might find out that it was merely a natural interest in a broken fire engine. Actually the objectives of such a first interview with a child are simply those of establishing a relationship of confidence by whatever means are given us, and in observing those tendencies within the child which are brought into play in this new and strange situation for whatever value they hold in estimating the character of his disorder.

Every child reacts in unique fashion to this first meeting with a caseworker. If he feels endangered by this strange situation into which he is thrust, he will defend himself against this danger in ways that are characteristic for him and of the greatest importance for us, both in evaluating his behaviour and in bringing him into a relationship with us.

Ellen, ten, is a constant daydreamer in school. Her teachers complain that she can't settle down to do her work. She is without friends, without any special interests. Ellen is in no sense a problem child in her foster home. She is a very 'good' child and displays great affection toward the foster parents with whom she has lived for four years. Her teachers and foster parents are puzzled.

In the first interview with the caseworker Ellen is immediately chatty, quite frankly tells the caseworker she has difficulty in school and then, quite unexpectedly, draws an idealized picture of the caseworker under which she writes, 'I love Miss Thomas' (the caseworker). Now we might count this as a triumph of relationship for Miss Thomas except that we know this is a most unusual reaction in a first interview with a child. Miss Thomas accepts the compliment pleasantly and without comment, then keeps her eyes open for some clues.

Later in the interview Ellen invents a drama with the puppets in which a little girl is very bad; she lies, talks back to her elders, and has secrets she will not tell her mother. The caseworker begins to understand Ellen's demonstration of love for her and an essential trait in Ellen's character. For it can be seen that Ellen has surrendered her aggressive tendencies, particularly those directed against adults, in favour of a compliant, dutiful attitude accompanied by exaggerated demonstrations of love toward the feared adult.

When we consider Ellen's background and a history of repeated placements because of behaviour problems, we can understand how she made her adjustment to this foster home. Her fear that her aggression might cause her to lose these loved foster parents as she had lost others was a factor in the transformation of these tendencies into their opposite – exaggerated love such as she employed with the caseworker. This major defensive operation was not entirely successful, however, for we see in the inability to do school work and the preoccupation with daydreams, that so much energy is required to keep these bad impulses in check that there is little left at the disposal of the psychic apparatus for the activity of learning.

In the first interview she does not know what the caseworker will do about her learning difficulties. She only knows that she has displeased her beloved foster parents on this score. She knows that, in the past, adult displeasure has led to rejection and replacement, often through the offices of a nice lady like Miss Thomas. In this new situation of danger she defends herself in characteristic fashion – she propitiates the dragon through a declaration of love.

This type of diagnosis is immediately useful to the caseworker. It is true that Ellen hints at naughty secrets that a little girl withholds from her mother, but this is of no immediate value to the caseworker, who is obliged to make certain judgments regarding the depth and severity of this disorder in order to make suitable treatment plans for the child.

Ellen's caseworker is concerned with these larger patterns. She wants to know the extent to which these defensive operations of the ego have made inroads into the personality structure. She wants to know their strength and malleability in order to know where and how modification of these trends can be carried out. We can compare this task with that of the architect who is called in for advice on the remodelling of a structure. He must judge the existing structure in terms of the strength of its materials and its points of weakness but he need not tear down the walls and rip up the flooring in the course of his survey; he can judge by external signs.

This brings us to a next point regarding the important work of the caseworker in early diagnosis of childhood disorders. It goes without saying that the diagnostic study of a child which is undertaken in order to make suitable treatment or environmental plans requires the broadest and deepest kind of understanding and equipment on the part of the caseworker. We have borrowed largely from the field of psychoanalysis for our understanding of stages of libidinal development and for our knowledge of neurotic symptom-formation. The significant psychoanalytic developments in the field of ego-psychology, however, seem not to be widely understood by caseworkers. Yet the whole process of social study and diagnosis is dependent upon a knowledge of ego-psychology. Recently in an address to psychiatrists, Dr Richard Sterba made certain remarks that I feel are specially pertinent for our field as well. He pointed out that in the past thirty years developments in the area of ego-psychology have made certain changes in the attitude of the psychiatrist in diagnostic interviews with patients. He said:

If we have to evaluate a patient today from a diagnostic therapeutic standpoint in an interview situation, we do not rely to such an extent on the symptomatology which he reports to us. Almost automatically we observe the patient's general behaviour, the peculiarities of his attitude toward us, his mannerisms and the mode and inflection of his speech. As we are aware of all these manifestations we use them for evaluation of the neurotic trends which permeate the behaviour, for they indicate to the experienced therapist the extent and the manner in which the neurosis afflicts the total personality and therefore the character.[1]

In the case of Ellen which we have briefly cited we are less interested in the fact that she daydreams – which is not in itself significant – than in the fact that her fantasies inhibit a normal ego-function, learning. We are less interested in the fact that she has aggressive fantasies and daydreams (which are allowable to any

[1] Unpublished manuscript.

child) than the fact that the ego of this child must deal with aggression in a specific way which is unsatisfactory and which leads to breakdown of an ego-function; the specific way, as we have already mentioned, is the transformation of the aggressive impulses into their opposite.

Another case which illustrates the uses of ego-psychology in evaluating a disorder of childhood caused us some concern a year and a half ago in a social agency. The case of eleven-year-old Eddie was brought in for discussion at a staff conference in the family agency. Three months earlier Eddie had come to the attention of the agency in connection with its camp programme. A school principal had asked that he be considered for placement at a clinical camp that is one of the valued resources of the agency. The reason: Eddie acted peculiarly in school. He would often burst out in classrooms and children's groups with bizarre and uncalled-for statements about death. The principal knew that a younger sister had died of leukaemia almost a year previously. As a matter of fact a great deal of newspaper publicity had been given to the child in the last months of her illness. The parents of Eddie had been deeply depressed since the little girl's death and there was still an atmosphere of mourning in the house. The parents continued to talk about the little girl to visitors, telling of her beauty and cleverness. There was one other child in the family, a girl two years younger than Eddie.

Eddie spent four weeks at the clinical camp, following which we obtained a report of the staff's observations. We saw that Eddie used every opportunity to bring in the tragic story of his sister. He appeared upset at the mention of death and once, after a church service that reminded him of his sister's funeral, he spoke of his own death and where he would like to be buried. On one occasion when the children were talking about murder stories, Eddie said quite seriously, 'If you want to hear about a murder story I'll tell you about the death of my sister.' This was evidently a slip, and a moment later he was remorseful. He then began to talk about his sister in heaven. When he looked up at the clouds, he said, he could sometimes see his sister sitting at the feet of Jesus. He described his sister as she looked in her coffin. The camp staff expressed something of the same concern for Eddie as had the principal of the school.

Admittedly this kind of preoccupation with death suggests pathology. We almost feel that we need very little more information to justify a recommendation for direct treatment. In our staff conference we investigated further the meaning of his symptoms. In a serious neurotic disorder with obsessional preoccupation with death we would find such manifestations as withdrawal, depression, inhibition, or turning inward of aggressive impulses, sometimes hypochondriacal complaints, or rituals and compulsive symptoms to ward off death or injury to the self. Yet as we examined the camp record further we saw that Eddie was capable of strong positive attachments to adults in the camp; he showed a lively interest in camp activities; he was able to engage in typical rough-housing with other campers. This was puzzling and certainly called for some modification of our views. We decided that the preoccupation with death had not invaded the total personality of this child. The ego was not restricted in its functioning. We combed the record for signs of pathological mechanisms in other areas of ego-functioning – and found none. We concluded that his preoccupation with death, because its sphere of operation was so limited and confined, was probably not obsessional in the clinical sense. 'What is this, then?' we asked ourselves.

We began to think of other factors. We thought of the long mourning of the parents, the atmosphere of death in this household, and the withdrawal of the parents from their two living children. We thought of the way in which the dead became sanctified and how this little daughter who had been unexceptional as a live little girl had become saintly, good, beautiful, and clever since her death. We thought of what it meant to a modest, workaday family in a small community to achieve fame and much newspaper publicity because it had a little girl dying of leukaemia.

In a real sense Eddie was placed in competition with his dead sister, but this competition was more devastating than anything he had known when the little sister was alive. He had nothing to offer that would compare with this spectacular illness and death. It might be, then, that his rather frequent and startling allusions to the dead sister and to the subject of death were his poor attempts to bring to himself some of the awesome respect that is given the dead and dying, to make himself important in the eyes of others through impressing himself upon them as the brother of a little girl who died of leukaemia. Such speeches also may have served another purpose; by sanctifying the dead sister he allayed some of his guilt about her death. This is suggested in the slip about his sister's 'murder'. We did not, however, feel that it was necessary for us to dwell too much on the problem of Eddie's guilt feelings, since guilt after a death is not in itself pathological. We have already seen that his guilt feelings had not created serious neurotic mechanisms in Eddie.

Considering all these things, beginning with our appraisal of a basically intact ego in this child and the circumstantial factors that had played a specific role in his preoccupation with death, the staff recommended that no direct treatment be attempted with Eddie but that our casework efforts be directed toward the parents in an effort to help them achieve some recognition of his problems.

Eddie's parents, both serious and concerned people, came to grips with their own feelings about the death of a loved child and their responsibility to the living children. When they recognized and grew concerned about the effects of their mourning upon Eddie as well as upon their other child, they brought about important changes in the home and in their relationship to the boy. As the atmosphere of the home became more normal, as Eddie discovered himself to be once more a valued child with his ghostly competitor put at rest, we saw dramatic changes in him. He became a normally cheerful and busy little boy, showed unexpected talent for taking on responsibility, and gratified his parents tremendously by his change from a listless and fretful member of the family to an independent, even boisterous, youngster. He never became a star at school – the little dead sister had always been a better student – but we learned that Eddie was actually a little limited intellectually and the best he could do was 'C' work. An understanding teacher and the parents accepted this limitation and helped Eddie achieve a feeling of importance for those other things that he did well, particularly in the area of mechanical skills. The stories about death and leukaemia stopped somewhere along the way. Now, a year and a half later, Eddie continues to function very well.

The case of Eddie illustrates a kind of casework which we speak of as 'environmental'. We see that an understanding of ego-psychology was indispensable to the casework staff in making an important decision regarding the type of treatment to be employed in a specific case. Had we considered the problem only from the point of view of the symptoms presented by Eddie we should have certainly felt that direct treatment of the child was indicated. But when the symptom is seen relatively and when the diagnostic eye of the caseworker is trained on the total configuration of ego-functioning and environmental influences, the significance of the symptom changes immediately. Here, an environmental approach to the problem was diagnostically prescribed.

8
Some aspects of casework with children
2. Helping with critical situations

Social Casework, vol. 33, no. 10, December 1952

Selma Fraiberg

Handling a specific problem with a particular known child is the focus of Selma Fraiberg's second paper. The social worker is leader of a group of eleven- and twelve-year-olds, one of whose members, Danny, a rejected, unwanted boy, is thought to be responsible for the theft of some equipment. Because she already has a relationship with him, the worker can open an immediate discussion about stealing without any preliminary small talk. In recognizing underlying worries, tension is reduced and the boy is helped to face the reality of his home circumstances and school. As a result, Danny experiences considerable relief; he is more responsive to the worker and there is no further stealing.

Some of the problems involved in the initial meeting of case-worker and child and in the use of the diagnostic or study period in casework with children were discussed in the first section of this paper. At this point we turn to another important area of casework with children. Many typical casework tasks involve one or two interviews with a child client for the purpose of dealing with a critical situation in his life. Thus, the placement worker may find it necessary to see a child because of a specific difficulty in the foster home, for discussion of a new placement, or possibly for preparation of the child for a tonsillectomy. The school social worker may have to interview a child about a classroom difficulty. The institutional caseworker may be called on to see one of her charges because of a theft or a fire-setting incident. Sometimes the caseworker is already acquainted with the child (this is particularly true, of course, in placement or institutional work) and he does not have to deal with the problem of establishing a new relationship, but he does face the special problems that come with confronting a child with a painful reality or in dealing with the guarded feelings of a child who feels he is 'on the spot'. In such instances, we are still not dealing with problems of casework treatment or therapy with the child but rather with a casework approach to critical events in a child's life. We do not exaggerate, I am sure, if we consider that our handling of such interviews with a child may profoundly influence his management of the critical event, his attitude toward his own problems and their solution, and even the course of his future development.

Because such encounters between caseworker and child occur frequently in casework agencies, it may be interesting for us to examine an interview with a child which involves the handling of a crisis – in this case, stealing. This material is taken from the record of a therapy group for boys of eleven and twelve years of age. The group leader was a trained caseworker who often found occasion to supplement her group handling of incidents with interviews with an individual child.

For several weeks there had been stealing in the group. A number of important items of equipment and many materials had disappeared. Finally, through many signs, the leader knew that Danny and Bill were chiefly involved in these thefts. When she was certain of the fact, she took both boys aside after a meeting, told them quietly that she wanted to talk with them privately about some of the missing items in the playroom and asked them to see her in her office on a specified day.

Even in this brief talk the attitude of each boy toward his stealing was evident. Bill had a 'Who? Me?' look written on his face and was well prepared with alibis; Danny looked shifty and uncomfortable although he made no admission of taking things. Formerly Danny had had a good relationship with the leader and it was not until the stealing began in the past few weeks that he had begun to avoid her. She already knew that Bill was the initiator and seducer in mischief and petty crime and that Danny was a willing partner who lacked boldness and cunning of his own but became daring and aggressive when he obtained a suitable partner. The boys were friends at school as well as in the group. Both had histories of stealing; Danny's seemed more sporadic while Bill's was a well-established pattern. Danny was living in the home of a maternal grandmother under supervision of a child-care agency which had earlier placed him in foster homes. His own parents were divorced and his mother had virtually abandoned him and his brother.

On the day of the scheduled interview Bill was ill. The worker had wanted to see the two boys together first and then have separate interviews with them. As it turned out, however, only Danny was able to come in for his interview. The following material is excerpted from the record:

Danny arrived early for his appointment. His face was streaked with dirt and his hair hung down into his eyes. He assumed a jaunty, unruffled manner. He said he couldn't find Bill. I said I had heard from Bill's mother that he was ill today. I commented it was too bad that Bill wasn't here but Danny and I could talk anyway. I suggested that maybe Danny understood why I had asked him to come in. He shifted uncomfortably. I said I knew that Danny and Bill had been taking things from the clubroom and so I thought it would be a good thing if we could get together and talk about this. He answered, 'Yes,' in a low voice.

I wondered what things Danny had taken. Danny hesitated. 'Well, sandpaper,' he said feebly. (Obviously the least valuable of the things he had taken.) 'And some glue and some airplane stuff, and some other stuff that I can't remember,' he went on. 'Bill took some scissors and some knives and he took lots of big things.' Then Danny was struck by his disloyalty to his friend. 'I don't really know,' he said. 'I don't know exactly what.'

I wondered whether Danny had taken things from other places and from other people too. He turned his head away. 'Yes,' he said. 'But,' he added, 'not big things.' I said little things could be important too. Like the things that Danny had taken from the club. It meant that other boys weren't able to use those things. Danny looked up at me gravely. 'Guess so,' he admitted in a low voice.

Then I said, 'You know, Danny, I like you a lot. And this makes me kind of worried because I do like you. It makes me think that if you do these things, and if you get yourself into jams and you steal, that maybe there's something bothering you. When boys do things like that it sometimes means that they're worried about something.' 'Worry?' said Danny, as if he had never heard the word before. 'Well, I worry about camp. I worry that maybe I can't go on account of my eyes. I had to go to the clinic about my eyes. And maybe they'll be so worse that I won't be able to go to camp this summer.'

[Now the worker understood. The entire club was going to be sent to camp by the agency that sponsored the group therapy project. Danny obviously felt that, now that he had stolen, his chances for camp had ended.]

I said I didn't know about that. I didn't really believe that needing glasses would keep a fellow out of camp. But I felt that maybe Danny meant that he was worried that I would be mad at him and not let him go to camp. Danny immediately looked up. 'That's what I was worrying about,' he said. I said I was not going to punish Danny. There was no reason why he should not go to camp. I wanted him to go to camp very much. A look of profound relief came over his face. Then I said, 'Was that the only thing you were worried about, Danny?'

'No,' Danny said, 'you see my grandma isn't going to keep my brother and me no more.' It cost him a lot to bring this out. Then he went on. 'Teddy and me, we live with my grandma. My mother and dad are divorced. So now my grandma says she isn't going to keep us no more and Miss Miller [caseworker at the placement agency], she's going to take us to a home. Once me and Teddy lived in a home. The lady didn't like me. She was real strict. You couldn't make no noise and you always had to put your things away. You had to come straight home from school and you couldn't play marbles on the way. And when you came home you couldn't even make yourself a jelly sandwich.' This last was somehow the most unbearable. Danny began to cry quietly.

[The worker had not known about the new placement plans although she had known for some time that a new placement might be considered eventually.]

I said, 'So it's pretty tough, isn't it, Danny? Now you don't know what'll happen. You don't know whether you'd like the new people or whether they'd like you?'

'I think all the time,' Danny said, 'I think that maybe it'll be a place where they won't like me. And then it won't be no better than at my grandma's. And maybe it'll be better if I just stay with my grandma. She don't like me. She don't like me because I stayed with my mother when I was a baby and my grandma always took care of Teddy. She don't like me because I like my mother. She says my mother is a bum. She likes Teddy best. When Teddy and me have a fight she always says that it's my fault. Teddy's stuff can lay around all the time and she don't say nothing. She always gets mad at me. When my stuff lays around she throws it out. I saved some money for a game and my grandma threw it in the dustbin. I s'pose she threw it in by mistake though. She says she wishes I was never born. She says I'm bad. She says I'm the trouble maker and I'm the cause of all her trouble. She says I'm good for nothing.'

'Do you think you're bad, Danny?' I asked. 'S'pose so,' Danny said briefly. 'Why?' I asked. 'Because I fight. And I always get into trouble. And – you know.' 'Yes,' I said, 'I think sometimes you do get into trouble and you do things you feel sorry for afterwards. But I don't think you're a bad boy, Danny.' I do not recall that Danny responded to this in any way. But he continued to tell me more stories about the home.

'Yesterday my grandma hit me with the stick because I was fighting with Teddy. Sometimes she's nice to us. I s'pose she really likes us sometimes. But she don't like me. I wished I had a family and then I wouldn't have so much trouble. I wished I had something to play with. My grandma don't have no money to buy Teddy and me anything to play with. And any time I get anything she says it's junk and she throws it out.'

I said, 'Danny, is that why you steal things? Because you figure if people don't give you things, you'll take them?' Danny made no answer. I said that I felt, too, that boys should have things to play with. Miss Miller, I was sure, felt the same way. These were things that Danny could talk about with Miss Miller and I knew that she would try to get him some of the things he wanted.

Then I asked, 'Danny, do you know what Miss Miller is there for?' and he answered promptly, 'To help me.' And that meant, I pointed out, that some of these things that Danny was so worried about and some of the things that Danny wanted, Miss

Miller could help him with. He could talk to her about these things.

Danny continued to tell me more stories. At school, he said, he had a teacher who made him ashamed before the whole class because he had dirty hands. I said that I knew how that could feel; it was awful to feel ashamed before other people, other kids especially. It was better, I thought, for grown-ups and children to talk about these things privately as we do here. 'Yes,' Danny said, 'that's what Miss Miller does too. We always talk private. Like if Teddy and me come down to the office we each see her private.'

Again Danny brought up his fear of the foster home and the fact that 'they' wouldn't like him. He concluded, 'I never stayed with anyone who liked me.' I asked, 'Who do you feel does like you, Danny?' He replied, 'My mother, I think. And my dad. Well, he used to but I don't know if he still does. And my aunt.' He was silent after he recited this miserable little list. 'And you know that I like you, don't you, Danny?' I asked. 'Sure,' Danny said, but then he added kindly, 'but you ain't in my family.'

Later on, as we talked, I asked Danny how he had felt last Thursday when I had talked with him and Bill about their stealing. 'I was mad,' he said, 'I wasn't going to come back. I thought to myself, "She said I took tools. And I didn't take tools." '

I pointed out that I had not said he took tools. 'I know,' he said, 'that's just the way I was thinking. Then afterward, Bill and me, we played marbles. Then Bill said he felt sick and he went home.'

Suddenly there came over Danny a wave of feeling. 'Bill, he made me spend money I saved up. I wished I didn't listen to him. Then I could of had something. Bill he's always getting into trouble. Like at school. We ain't supposed to go into only one door. Bill he always wants to go into the other doors. He's always taking chances. And Bill he talks back to the teachers. He says, "They can't do nothing." '

Danny continued, 'Once Danny Peters said he didn't want to take no chances and Bill said he was a sissy. Just scared.' I asked, 'Just because he didn't want to take a silly chance and get into trouble?' 'Yah!' was Danny's reply.

'I think taking chances like that is kind of dumb,' I remarked. 'Sure,' Danny agreed. I said, 'When Bill says that to you, what can you say?' 'Tell him I'm not taking no chances,' he said. I suggested, 'Sure, I'd say, "Not me. I'm not dumb."'

Danny's next remark was, 'Bill he gets into lots of trouble.' 'I know,' I said, 'I like Bill but I'm afraid he's going to get into a pack of trouble by doing these things. Bill does need someone to help him.'

It was nearly time to end our interview. I said I was very glad that we had this chance to talk. Said Danny, 'I got a lot of things off my chest.'

Danny was at the door now. He turned to me and said shyly, 'You know that boat you helped me with? It was the best boat I ever made.' 'It was a swell boat,' I said, 'and you made it too!' 'Sure,' Danny agreed, 'but I knew how to make it good because you helped me.'

In this interview with Danny certain typical problems in casework with children come to the foreground. With an adult client the caseworker usually grants the 'right of self-determination'; with a child he must assume a different kind of responsibility. He must actively step in at times like this and interfere with 'self-determination' of a certain kind. He must bring about a sense of responsibility for acts if his client is of an age and disposition that do not normally give rise to social feelings. Most unpleasant of all for the caseworker is the task of confronting a child with his juvenile crime.

In this interview we notice that the worker opened the discussion with a frank acknowledgment of the fact that she knew Danny had been taking things. She did not preface this with small talk and she did not try to make it easy for Danny. Earlier we spoke of the necessity for inviting a child's confidence in the caseworker and deliberately putting him at ease, and this bald opening of the caseworker seems to contradict everything we have discussed. But does it? First of all, this worker was known to her client as a group leader, and a good relationship had existed for months before the stealing began, at which time Danny became evidently less interested in her good opinion of him. The bald opening of the caseworker leads in this instance to a simple acknowledgment on the part of two people who know each other that something which concerns both of them and which is known to both of them must be discussed in the open. Since Danny knows precisely the reason for the interview, small talk is pointless. Also, the worker in this instance does not want to put her client at ease. She feels that it is best that he feel guilty for what he has done. She knows that he does not ordinarily feel much guilt about his delinquencies but here she is banking on her formerly good and warm relationship with Danny to cause him some discomfort and guilt. Clearly, without such an earlier relationship such an approach might bring hostility toward a nosy stranger, rather than guilt. She deliberately shows her concern for Danny. Because of his discomfort, Danny's attitude toward his delinquencies may change. Also, in order to handle the stealing episode at all with Danny, she must bring him to some acknowledgment of responsibility for his acts.

The worker has another objective in this interview. She wants to understand as far as possible the meaning of the stealing episodes so that she can handle these acts as symptoms. If the total picture seems serious, the worker may recommend to Danny's agency that treatment be sought for him. If, on the other hand, the stealing is largely a reaction to external circumstances and pressures, the worker may suggest to the agency, on the basis of her interest, that appropriate remedial measures be carried out. Therefore, soon after opening up the subject of stealing the worker directs Danny's attention to the fact that stealing is a symptom. She tells him that when boys do things of this sort it often means they are worried about something.

But what is Danny's response to this? He first denies any worry and then lamely expresses his fear that he will not be able to go to camp because of his eyesight. He fears that the worker will punish him for the stealing by not permitting him to go to camp. As soon as this is handled with Danny and he is assured that the worker actually wants him to go to camp, the interview takes a new turn. Now he can tell the worker about his big worry. His grandmother is not going to keep him any more. Miss Miller is going to take him and his brother to a home.

Actually Danny has no reason to expect that he will not be punished for his stealing, nor does any other child who comes to us following a delinquent episode. Danny can only expect that the worker will act like any other adult and he is already prepared

with the full battery of defences and alibis. His jaunty, uncon-
cerned manner at the beginning of the interview is part of this
defence. His admission to the theft of some trifles is the kind of
compromise confession he feels it is necessary to make. Even
though he knows this worker very well he still cannot measure
how she will react under these conditions, what she does to boys
when they steal. Only when he understands that she will not
punish, when he experiences the relief of knowing he will go to
camp, does he really perceive that her interest in his stealing is
different from that of other adults. She wants to know *why* a boy
steals, what worries make him steal. So he tells her.

As he talks we are impressed by the acuteness of this child's
dilemma. He knows he is unloved and he is told he is bad. If there
are no rewards for 'being good' in Danny's life, if one is considered 'bad' anyway, why shouldn't he be bad? And he is deprived, terribly deprived in every meaning of the word. He is
without love, without meaningful relationships to any adult,
without family, without possessions. As the worker suggests to
him at one point, it is as if his defence for his stealing lies in the
simple rationale, 'If people don't give me things, then I will take
them.'

Our experience with children tells us that this type of stealing is
perhaps the least complicated in the long category of stealing
types. Such youngsters as Danny often give up their stealing when
we are able to provide meaningful relationships for them, when
the minuses are changed to pluses on the human relations ledger.

It may be worth while to mention that Danny's partner in
crime, Bill, has far more complicated motives in his stealing. His
defence against guilt feelings and against meaningful object relationships tells of a more entrenched delinquent attitude. Nor is
Bill, strictly speaking, a deprived youngster. His stealing has to do
with rivalry with a stepfather, with seductive attitudes on the part
of his mother, altogether a more complex pattern. An interview
with Bill would not be so simple as the one with Danny. A more
developed delinquent type of youngster would protect his anxieties and inner feelings from the prying caseworker. The manner
in which Danny surrenders his defensive attitude when the non-
punitive and sympathetic attitude of the caseworker finally
reaches him, tells us that this is not a very complicated delinquent.

We are interested in the way in which Danny understands this novel approach (for him) to his stealing. In his outpouring he mentions that a teacher once made him ashamed before his whole class because of his dirty hands. He seems to be saying thanks to the caseworker for not betraying him and humiliating him before the group. He must never have known before this experience where a boy's 'badness' is handled in an interview, where stealing is seen as a symptom that 'something is wrong inside'. He confesses, too, that before this interview and at the time of the group meeting when the worker privately spoke to him and Bill, he had been angry at the accusation and had decided he would not come back to the club.

Finally comes the wave of feeling against Bill and the way in which he tempted Danny into delinquent acts. We recall that earlier Danny was loyal to Bill and was careful not to betray him. In the outpouring now against Bill, Danny tells us that in the course of the interview something has changed in his attitude not only toward Bill but toward his own delinquencies. It is as if Bill represents his 'bad part' and in the outburst against Bill and his repudiation of Bill we see how he shows the wish, for this moment anyway, to repudiate his own 'badness', his own inner temptations. The worker chooses to support this attitude in Danny and expresses concern for Bill and what will happen to him if such things continue.

Earlier we spoke of the difficulty that children have in understanding what we mean by 'help'. At the end of this interview with Danny we understand that he was giving shy thanks to the worker for her help. He spoke of the boat she had helped him make, we remember, the best he ever made. 'But I knew how to make it good because you helped me.' He seemed to understand 'help' here. The question remains whether he would have understood it earlier. For the experience in the interview made 'help' concrete and significant where earlier 'help' would have been a word without positive content to this child who, like so many of our children, had never known what this kind of help could mean.

The outcome of this interview was a good one. There were no further stealing episodes in the group. Danny's relationship to the group leader was again a warm one and he sought many opportunities to be with her and to talk with her, though not necessarily about 'private' things. The worker, of course, shared this interview with Danny's agency so that this material could be used in planning for Danny.

In every agency where caseworkers work with children, the worker carries the weight of the responsibility for making critical decisions for children and their families. Not only must we make judgments regarding the treatment of a wide variety of childhood disorders but we are often called upon to make decisions or recommendations regarding placement outside the home. We are, willingly or not, great manipulators of a child's life. This is an awesome kind of responsibility, and perhaps an attitude of awe toward such undertakings is a proper one for us. We need to feel inadequate before the magnitude of these tasks.

It is this responsibility that I want to talk about most of all. I feel that there are few professions in which are found such ideals, such dedication, and such seriousness of intent as in social work. Our errors, when we make them, are rarely from malice, or neglect, or self-interest. Surely we can be forgiven, I say to myself, if we err in our judgments sometimes. But then my thoughts travel back to the errors and the source of the errors and their consequences, and I feel bound to speak of them. For these errors, these mistakes in judgment, affect human lives profoundly, sometimes irrevocably. In the case of a child, a mistaken judgment can inalterably change the course of a life. Therefore, let us speak honestly to each other about one of the chief sources of error in our professional work with children. It is not lack of love and sympathy for children, or lack of proper concern for our charges. We abound in these virtues. I believe that the chief source of error in our work with children is the equipment we bring to our work. We need to know so much in order to help a child build a life, to help his parents build his life, and to rebuild a child's life when it has been destroyed. We need to know everything one can know today about the deepest sources of disease and health in the mental life of childhood. The most commonplace, everyday casework task requires the most thorough training in psychological development of the child, the richest possible experiences in work with normal and abnormal children under varied circumstances, with varied age ranges.

I do not know how this equipment and training for caseworkers will be obtained in the casework education of the future. But it seems to me that we must begin with an appreciation of the seriousness of the caseworker's responsibility for children. It is a fact that there are no elementary tasks in casework just as there are no elementary psyches among our clients; hence there is no place for an elementary education in human psychology for the caseworker. Already there are gratifying changes in the programmes of schools of social work. We no longer believe that the psychiatric social worker must have a broader education in psychology than the family caseworker, the child welfare worker, the medical caseworker. When we have achieved the broadest possible education for social workers (I speak here of the field of child casework) we shall do more than reduce the margin of error in our judgments; I think we shall begin to see the realization of an old dream in which social workers will be able to do preventive casework with children and their families on a scale not yet thought possible.

These two papers, nos 7 and 8, were presented by Selma Fraiberg at the National Conference of Social Work, Chicago, in May 1952, at the time when she was Consultant in Casework with Children, Down River Consultation Service, Wyandotte, Michigan. Most of her professional career has, however, been spent in University teaching, first as a lecturer in Child Development then, since 1968, as Professor of Child Psychoanalysis at the University of Michigan. Her present research is concerned with young blind children. She has written widely for professional journals in the social work and psychiatric fields. Her book, The Magic Years, *about understanding and handling the problems of early childhood, published in England in 1968 by Methuen, has been translated into several languages.*

9
The understanding caseworker

New Society, 1 August 1963

Olive Stevenson

At a time when the relevance of dynamic psychology to social work is again under discussion, Olive Stevenson's article is particularly pertinent. Although not primarily concerned with children, it has not been shortened because it contains so much interesting material for the social worker.

A car journey provides the setting for communication with a child. Ten-year-old Anne, being moved because of the breakdown of her foster home, is very upset and needs to cry. How often in such situations have we been tempted to comfort a child by diverting attention to happier, 'safer' subjects? In this case, the worker allows, indeed encourages, Anne to dwell on the sadness; on her feelings of loss; of being abandoned and bereft; she is helped to express pain and anger. The worker is thereby involved in the girl's unhappiness and shares it with her. By experiencing this grief in an intense way, Anne will be better able to relinquish what she has lost and will be freer to make new relationships.

In 1959, Barbara Wootton's *Social Science and Social Pathology* was published and current theory in social casework was strongly attacked. The social worker 'has no need to pose as a miniature psychoanalyst or psychiatrist. . . . Rather than search for something deeper underneath when her help is sought in external practical emergencies, the social worker would do better to look for something more superficial on top when she is confronted with problems of behaviour.' With this open declaration of war, social workers all over the country took out their weapons; but unaccustomed as a group to open aggression and unused to the cut and thrust of academic life, they mostly found their weapons rusty or blunt and, putting them back, just got on with the job. There were effective comments in various social work journals; but, by and large, these did not reach the ears of intelligent people on the fringes of social work.

One finds therefore still a lingering uncertainty as to the justice of Lady Wootton's comments even among those who are fundamentally sympathetic to social casework. Those who are less sympathetic, both to casework and to psychoanalysis, have used Lady Wootton's merciless exposure of the vague and pretentious jargon in which some social work writing is couched to obscure the fundamental issue – of what use is dynamic psychology to social caseworkers? The purpose of this article is to examine and illustrate the contribution that such theory can make to social caseworkers in this country in their everyday tasks.

Kathleen Woodruffe in her book *From Charity to Social Work* aptly remarks: 'If, in the United States, there was a psychiatric deluge in the 1920s, in England during the same period there was nothing more than a trickle which even though it was to grow in the following decades, never reached the majestic swell of its American counterpart.' While it is essential to realize the interaction of economic, sociological and psychological factors in the problems with which a social worker is presented, it would be sad indeed if at our present stage of development, we turned away from the contribution of dynamic psychology to the understanding and handling of complex situations when it is only beginning to be appreciated in Great Britain.

It is not my object to discuss the theoretical basis or scientific validity of psychoanalytic theory. Few subjects point up more clearly the gulf between the research worker and the practitioner, for despite its many unproven assumptions, this body of theory has offered much concrete help to social workers in carrying out their tasks. There are three ways in which this help is offered:

First, by offering hypotheses concerned with the influence of past experiences on present behaviour and – closely related – of the ways in which unconscious feelings influence behaviour. This permits deeper understanding of the problems involved.

Second, by enabling social workers to formulate a realistic plan for those they seek to help, taking into account the above factors. If these are left unconsidered, the help given to the person may be ineffective.

Third, by centring attention on the actual processes of an interview. A social caseworker pays attention to the currents of feeling between herself and the person she tries to help and uses these constructively for the benefit of the person.

It is important to distinguish between the theoretical content of the various schools of psychoanalysis and their therapeutic method. The first two of the above points are concerned with theoretical content, upon which any person who wants to help and understand others may draw; the third point is concerned with the method and it is here that there has been much misunderstanding, for the social caseworker is not seeking to imitate the method of the psychoanalyst but to borrow from his skills and techniques certain useful ideas and bend them to her purpose.

These three points are illustrated by the case material which follows, which has been chosen from the Child Care Service though in fact the principles apply to all social casework. Child care cannot be seen as a social work service which dabbles unnecessarily in people's private affairs or intimate emotions. Yet in carrying out her appointed task, the child care officer cannot possibly ignore the complex emotions of those she tries to help – they are forced upon her and every day she is confronted with puzzling behaviour and complicated situations which are most helpfully explained by dynamic psychology.

The following example illustrates such an everyday problem.

The child care officer is sent for by irate foster parents. Jennifer is ten years old. She has been fostered since she was ten months old but in the early months of her life she was severely neglected. Now says the child care officer: 'No one can give her enough: she wants everything for herself.' At the time of the crisis, the foster mother is ill in bed, cared for by the grandmother. Granny asks Jennifer to go and fetch a traycloth for mummy's tray. Jennifer gets one out that she has embroidered and takes the tray up. She asks for the chocolates by the foster mother's bed, but is refused. She snatches the traycloth, rushes out and cuts it into small pieces with scissors.

In talking to the child care officer, it is evident that she sees this incident as the act of a child who is struggling towards 'giving' in relationship but because of her early experiences is still to a large extent at the mercy of her infantile, primitive feelings of an eye for an eye and a tooth for a tooth. Refused a chocolate, she has at once to destroy her gift to her foster mother. The situation is complicated by the illness of the foster mother and the anxiety this rouses in the child and the fact that she is taking food up to the foster mother and is refused food herself – this being one of the most sensitive areas for the deprived child who equates food and love.

This is how the child care officer explains it to herself; the background to such an explanation is to be found in Kleinian psychoanalytic theory. It is helpful in comprehending a strange episode which has hurt and puzzled the foster parents; and the child care officer will enable them to cope better with their feelings, and understand what they need to do for Jennifer, because she sees a meaning in it and can explain something of the problem to them. The important point here is that the child care officer's whole approach to the situation is altered by her understanding. Less baffled herself, she conveys a certain security to those she seeks to help.

These and comparable problems are commonplace. Trained child care officers or those who, without formal training, have educated themselves, find in developmental psychology a theory that makes some sense out of what would otherwise seem nonsense.

The following is the case of Mrs Cartwright. The child care officer is asked to visit because Mrs Cartwright wants her expected baby to be adopted. A previous illegitimate child has been adopted. Mrs Cartwright is thirty-seven years old, has been married for a year. She is a big woman but (in the words of the child care officer) 'somehow soggy, and shapeless'. 'She has large and somewhat clumsy hands.' Her husband seems to have opted out of the situation and is leaving the decision to his wife though it is clear he does not really want the baby to be adopted. These are extracts from interviews with Mrs Cartwright.

First visit. Immediately she saw me Mrs Cartwright began to cry. I suggested that she should sit down and tell me what was the matter, and she sat down in the chair and buried her face in her hands and said that she just would not be able to cope with this baby as she was not a good wife: she had only been married a year: she could not cook: and she was no good. . . . Mrs Cartwright went on to tell me that until last year she had lived at home with her mother. She was an only child and had never had to do anything for herself. She had gone out to work as a shop assistant, and her mother had done everything in the house. She told me how her mother used to wait for her when she got in in the evenings, and kneel down and take her shoes off and put her slippers on, and she never lifted a finger at home.

Until she married, she had never washed clothes, ironed, cooked or cleaned. . . . She could only just manage to keep things going now, and if she was forced to keep the baby she would be desperate and would do something silly. When I asked her about this, she said she might hit the baby, or do something to it, because she would hate it. . . . She became rather hysterical and seemed to be trying to force me into doing what she wanted. When she found that I did not respond to her crying and hysteria, she tried to reason with me on a much quieter level, but when this still did not extract from me a promise to take the baby, she began to bang on the arms of the chair, saying that she would be sick if I went on like this . . .

The child care officer paid two more home visits in which Mrs Cartwright behaved in much the same way. She then visited Mrs Cartwright in the hospital after the birth of the baby, which was premature and weighed $4\frac{1}{2}$ lb.

First of all she did not raise the question of the baby at all, merely saying that it was very kind of me to come and see her and that she was feeling miserable. However, after we had talked about this, she said that she supposed I had come to see her about the baby. I said that I had heard that she was in hospital and thought that I ought to just come and tie the ends up as I understood from the almoner that she was going to take the baby home with her after all when it was discharged. Mrs Cartwright burst into sobs, saying that she wanted to take the baby home but that she hoped she would be able to cope. She is, I think, torn between the very real fear which she feels about handling the child, and the guilt which she would feel if she did not take the baby home. She told me that her husband had told her that she ought to take the baby home, and this was why she had changed her mind. She kept on saying what a little thing it was, and how she would never be able to manage, but also added that she would not rest if she had left the child in hospital or had her placed for adoption. . . . I asked her if she thought it would help if I visited her, although I could not promise to come on a regular basis. She grasped at this in a pathetically grateful way.

July home visit. As soon as Mrs Cartwright opened the door she said accusingly that it was about time that I came, she had waited for me all last week. I said that she had perhaps not received my letter telling her I would be on holiday. She only grunted at this and led the way into the living-room. The baby was lying in the pram in the window, crying and waving her arms. Mrs Cartwright turned the pram so that the child was out of sight, and I sat down on the other side of the room. Mrs Cartwright plucked a cigarette from the packet and lit it, with her hand shaking slightly. I said that I was glad to see her out of hospital. Her reply was a grunt, and a clicking of her lips, impatiently. I asked if she was feeling cross about my not being here last week. She replied that it was like me to be away when she needed me.

She began to cry, saying I knew perfectly well she was not going to be able to manage the baby and all the housework. Mr Cartwright was grumbling already because she thought he ought to do things, but *he* ought to do all the housework and then she could look after the baby. Would that help, did she think? She said that I would have to so something, she just could not manage. The baby must be placed for adoption. Who had suggested that? Her mother, she replied. I said non-committingly 'Oh, I see.' I said that this was a very serious matter. She said it was only a question of getting the baby away, then everything would be all right. I said that even if the baby was away she would have to cope with her own feelings. She said she wouldn't mind that, but when I pointed out that Mr Cartwright might throw up in her face that she had forced him into a position where he had to agree to adoption, she agreed rather sadly, but said that she couldn't cope with the baby, no matter what I said.

At this point she rose and picked up the baby from the pram, and after a moment deposited her rather summarily on my lap. The baby yelled at this treatment and Mrs Cartwright said that I could see how it was, the baby cried all the time, and she couldn't manage everything. It would be all right if someone else could be there all the time, but when she was on her own, she couldn't be expected to cope. She supposed I thought she ought to manage on her own, other women did, but she was different, she was always delicate, and if she didn't have some help, she would be ill. She couldn't be expected to manage, her mother said so. I said I could understand how difficult it was for her as she had always been so dependent on her mother, but I thought that perhaps if she took things gradually she might be surprised at what she could achieve. This brought another outburst of tears and Mrs Cartwright accused me of being 'hard'. (I felt rather defeated at this point and wondered if I *had* been hard) . . . She went on to say Mr Cartwright should not have made her pregnant, he knew she was delicate and her mother had told him that she ought not to have any children. She needed someone to help her, never mind about the baby. She then followed this by a series of demands that I should visit her often – daily or weekly – and when I would not tie myself down, she looked rather rebellious, then cried, then insisted that the baby was going to cry (she wasn't), picked her up and again deposited her on my lap, after a few moments. I said, 'You really are determined to give me this baby one way or another, aren't you?' She flushed quite visibly and said, 'Well, I can't manage, someone has got to look after her. I have told him that I can't manage and that I am going to make sure that you make some arrangements for the baby.' (Tears.)

I said that I thought that though she was terribly anxious about managing the care of the baby, at the same time there was a part of her that probably wanted to make a go of things and would feel horrible if I did take the baby. . . . I said that I would come and see her in a week's time and we could talk some more, if she thought this would help her. She asked could I come again this week – on Saturday – and I said I could not. 'Why not?' 'Because I do not work on Saturdays.' At this she pouted and said that she thought I ought to be able to stretch a point sometimes. I laughed and said that I wasn't willing to on this occasion because I thought she was trying to get her own way about something as I hadn't fallen in with her other plans. She insisted on pinning me down to a specific day next week. I got up, holding the baby, and asked where I should put her. She would not hold her, but insisted I put her in the pram.

Conclusion: I feel very worried about this case. I am worried that Mrs Cartwright is trying to force me into a replica of her managing mother and she is creating in me a desire to 'fix things up nicely'.

The sequel to this story is a happy one; Mrs Cartwright gained sufficient confidence in her capacities as a mother to keep the baby and to cope with it reasonably well. Gradually the child care officer stopped visiting and the health visitor supported Mrs Cartwright over the practical care of the baby. She rings up the child care officer occasionally to say 'everything is OK', and the child care officer comments 'she is really telling me she is being a good girl'.

It would be possible to go through the Cartwright case and use psychoanalytic terminology to discuss its content; the concepts of ambivalence, of transference and counter-transference – these and much more besides, integral to psychoanalytic theory, are there for all to see. The social caseworker does not need to use these terms or even necessarily to realize fully in conscious thought the debt she owes to such theory, and indeed it may be that the better the knowledge is integrated, the less obvious will be the connections. But if we watch the way the problem is tackled and recorded, we cannot doubt that the inferences of the theory inform and illumine her dealings with Mrs Cartwright. Her story described by many social workers would not reveal this kind of insight into the situation, which gives us the clues we need for understanding.

The child care officer sees quickly the connection between the presenting problem and Mrs Cartwright's relationship with her own mother, which has seriously undermined her confidence as a woman. But she sees even further the way in which Mrs Cartwright tries to place her in the same dominant, maternal role. She identifies the feeling of anxiety and 'the desire to fix things up nicely' which the woman rouses in her. Mrs Cartwright wishes the child care officer to be 'on tap' as her own mother had been – even on Saturday afternoons. She is angry that the child care officer goes on holiday – 'it's like you to be away when I need you' – this said to someone she has only met on three or four occasions.

In recognizing all this the child care officer avoids two pitfalls. She does not on the one hand fall in with Mrs Cartwright's demands, either by taking the action which would result in the adoption of the baby, or by visiting exactly when Mrs Cartwright wants her to. On the other hand, she does not allow herself to be riled by Mrs Cartwright's behaviour and reject with annoyance the woman who tries to manipulate her. In her relationship with Mrs Cartwright, she fosters the growth of independence.

Anyone who has had contact with the immature and hysterical personality such as we see in Mrs Cartwright will know that the pressure on the helping person to 'do something' is very great. Crisis feelings are catching and the likelihood of being forced into the action demanded by the other person is considerable.

The talk with Anne which follows shows us other ways in which dynamic psychology has influenced social casework but also shows clearly how the techniques of social casework differ from those of psychotherapy or psychoanalysis. Anne is ten years old and she has broken down in her foster home, where she has lived for seven years. She has been fostered with very staunch and rather rigid churchgoers and among other misdemeanours has caused distress to her foster mother by shouting 'bum and belly' at church meetings.

The child care officer feels that her outbursts are a reaction to the excessive rigidity and that the breakdown is due more to fundamental incompatibility than actual naughtiness on Anne's part. Anne is not very intelligent but lively and quick in her responses; she is small with 'buttony brown eyes'.

She leaned out of the car waving to Miss M as we went off and then sat down, saying nothing. I was having difficulty in negotiating heavy traffic and could not get even a look at her for a while. When I was able to I could see that tears were pouring down her face though she was very quiet about it and turning her head away from me. I drew the car to the side of the road and said that I expect she was feeling a bit sad. She nodded and did not protest when I put my arm around her and cuddled her. She began to cry more openly, saying that she was only crying because she was tired and was feeling sick. I sympathized and said I expected that it was a little bit because she was missing her Mummy and Daddy (foster parents). She nodded to this and said that Mummy said she wasn't to cry because she was a big girl and big girls didn't cry. I said that sometimes big girls did cry if they felt very sad and this sometimes made you feel a lot better. Things often hurt people very much inside and then they cried. She said she supposed it was all right so long as I didn't mind . . .

At lunch, I talked about what the children's home looked like, the names of all the people there, and the children who would be in her group. She wrapped my travelling rug around her shoulders, clutching a teddy bear and said she was going to sleep. She pretended to go to sleep, but obviously didn't and while she had her eyes shut managed to arrange herself across the seat so that her head was on my lap. She stayed there for a while then sat up, still wrapped in the rug, saying that this rug was magic and when you were wrapped in it, you could wish for anything and it came true. She asked what I wished for but when I suggested that she had first wish she said she was wishing for a nice house, ever so pretty, with a nice garden. I asked who lived in the house and she said a Mummy and Daddy and some little girls. The little girls were naughty sometimes. But their Mummy didn't mind a bit. She just said 'It's all right, my dear.' Nothing ever happened to them when they were naughty.

I said that perhaps she thought she had been naughty and her Mummy had been cross with her. She said airily that she thought she might go to sleep now. I said I thought perhaps she felt that her Mummy had been very cross and had sent her away. That wasn't so, she had come to be near her very own brother and she was not a naughty girl; I thought she was a very nice girl and very clever too. She asked if she could have a jelly baby and took one out of the box on the car shelf. I said she didn't seem to want to think about home. Anne said she didn't know what

I meant. I said I thought she was frightened to think about it because she was thinking she had been sent away. She hadn't been sent away because she was naughty, she was not a wicked girl. Anne still clutched the rug around her and said that she knew a boy who was very naughty and he had been put down a hole in the ground and then he went to Hell (awed sort of voice). I said I didn't believe there was a place like Hell – God didn't go around punishing people, He liked them. Anne looked doubtful about this but didn't question it.

She went on to talk about living in N, telling me about the children she knew, but carefully avoiding reference to home. I asked her one or two questions about the boys and Mr and Mrs H and each time she replied only in monosyllables. I asked her about the cats in the house and she began to explain that Mummy had brought one of these home, sticking at the word 'Mummy' but swallowing and then going on. I talked about her going back in holiday times to see the cats and the family and she seized this avidly and asked how long till the holidays, how would she get there? I explained that it was eight weeks and I would be taking her.

Anne finally fell asleep, and then when she woke appeared to be very depressed, saying that eight weeks was a terribly long time and I might forget. I encouraged her to talk about home and talked to her about the children's home and she finally said in quite a temper: 'I don't want to be sent away from home, I don't like that place we are going to and I want to go back to N, and I want to go *now*.' I said I knew it was hard and I knew she hated it and it made her feel all funny inside, but I would be there and I would see her quite often and I would help her all I could. She cried a little, saying, 'Please take me back now', but became a little calmer and finally settled down in the seat as close as she could get to me with her hand on my arm. I talked about her brother and said that he was terribly excited about seeing her and Anne began to show slight interest in this. She finally began to talk about seeing him in a pleased way and continued so to the end of the journey.

Philosophers and theologians and others have long known that there is relief in the acknowledgement of painful feeling and the psychoanalyst cannot claim a novel discovery. But in this record, one sees the worker confident in Anne's need to face this, not allowing her to escape from it and, even more important perhaps, able to deal with the impact of the child's grief on herself and not avoid the issue. In conversation the child care officer said – 'Years ago I would have said – look at the nice sheep in that field, and tried to cheer Anne up.' But here she does not let Anne take refuge in changing the subject when she says she might go to sleep now or asks for a jelly baby. She comforts the child but recognizes the need to keep the feeling open and flowing; her experience and knowledge will have shown her that if the feeling is dammed up, the child's pain, anger and resentment may effectively block the later adjustment, in this case to the children's home and to the foster home to which she was to return for holidays.

It is very clear in this record that the child care officer is no 'miniature psychoanalyst' for her concern is not to explore deeply unconscious fantasy – which she is nether trained nor employed to do – but rather to recognize, as it were, the little pieces of the iceberg which show above the surface in order to help the child handle better the realities of the situation. On this long car journey, the child care officer is deliberately bridging the gap between the past and the future by the purposive references to both. The child care officer knows that in children who move from one place to another the images of peoples and places are often blurred and disturbed by the feelings – of anger, of fear, of sadness, which surround them, and that these are often intense. The task is therefore to try to keep the reality of the situation alive and relatively unclouded by the fantasies. In order to do this, the child care officer must be alive to the significance of casual remarks or significant stories, such as Anne could tell when encouraged by the magic rug and the child care officer's interest. Dynamic psychology has focused attention on the detail of the interview and the worker who is sensitive and deft quickly sees her opportunity of using this; so that she does not, for example, fall into the error of 'having the first wish' and thus diverting attention from Anne.

It has been my intention to illustrate from these cases the ways in which a child care officer uses this kind of theory. It is not my intention to claim that this is the only ingredient of social casework in whatever setting it is practised. Behind the use of such theory must lie other kinds of knowledge and, above all, compassion and humility; otherwise there is no justification for its use. The most profound contribution that psychoanalytic theory makes to those who have really made it a part of themselves is that it destroys for ever the 'they-and-us' illusion.

Far from encouraging a subtle form of superiority, the social caseworker who has grasped the essentials of this realizes as never before the implications for herself. Such knowledge is in fact a protection to the person being helped, for it makes the caseworker far more aware of her own involvement in the problem. It is also a protection to the caseworker for it makes possible a degree of self-control based on genuine insight which limits, not her compassion, but her vulnerability to the painful situations to which she is constantly exposed.

Olive Stevenson began her professional career as a child care officer in Devon where she worked for four years. Following the Tavistock Clinic Advanced Social Casework Course she entered social work education, first at Bristol University and, since 1960, in the Oxford University Department of Social and Administrative Studies. In 1968, she was seconded by the University to the Supplementary Benefits Commission as their social work adviser and returned to the University in 1969 as Reader in Applied Social Studies.

10
Life for Kim

Case Conference, vol. 10, no. 10, April 1964

R O Prestage

'*Under all speech that is good for anything there lies a silence that is better*' – THOMAS CARLYLE

Emphasis has so far been on direct casework with children away from their homes. Mrs Prestage's article concerns a nine-year-old boy, Kim, who lives with his ambitious, professional parents and two siblings. He was unwanted and since birth has carried an insupportable load of his mother's projections. As a result of her own earlier experiences, she felt that her first child would be hostile and destructive. By the time he is referred to the Child Guidance Clinic he is unable to trust any adults, is spiteful and aggressive. The social worker unfolds a remarkable story of tenacity of purpose as she attempts to find a way to communicate with this withdrawn, solitary child. The importance of messages conveyed by the eyes is highlighted. She realizes that he acknowledges her presence because he watches her so closely as he proceeds for fourteen silent sessions to climb a tree. Her totally accepting attitude, sometimes at variance with her real feelings, results in better communication, often non-verbal, being established as they share activities.

When nine-year-old Kim first came to the Child Guidance Clinic because of his aggressive and spiteful behaviour, he presented a picture of dogged and hopeless misery. His world was an unfriendly, persecutory place and he had become adept at seeking out punishment for his angry and guilty thoughts. His initial contact with the clinic apparently did little to alleviate his suffering and may well have confirmed his opinion that there was no hope for him from the adult world, as he quickly transferred his gloomy attitude to the psychiatrist who, it should be noted, had the same surname as Kim. He made no attempt of any kind to relate and his depression was the more marked by contrast with the emotional health and gaiety of his two younger siblings.

Whilst their mother talked with the psychiatrist, I kept the three children company in the playroom. I was struck by Kim's rigid and inhibited stance as he stood aloof, watching the two-year-old David and six-year-old Ann gleefully immersed in the sand tray. He habitually stood with his right hand behind his back – for fear of what it might do, I wondered? I was aware of my own subjective reaction to this thin, knobbly boy when I found myself thinking how pathetically vulnerable and inchoate was the nape of his stiff little neck. In other words, our old friend the counter-transference was already at work. I was therefore sorry to learn that Kim denied all problems and sulkily refused any suggestion of therapy, turning his back on the clinic, metaphorically and literally, with all possible speed. The psychiatrist reported, 'this is a neurotic family situation in which aggression can only be expressed by such devious means as Kim employs. He is an intelligent boy but emotionally impoverished and lacking in spontaneity. He has no incentive to change the *status quo* and psychiatric intervention is not acceptable.'

His mother, a school teacher, who had initiated the referral herself, requested further interviews, and we arranged weekly sessions which the small David came to enjoy with all the zest and abandon of a cheerful two-year-old who finds a large and well-equipped playroom at his disposal. I suppose we become so accustomed to dealing with disturbed children in the clinic that, by comparison, I found this toddler's happy spontaneity greatly refreshing. His mother once described how he greeted the mention of my name at a meal with the association 'sand' and clambered purposefully out of his high chair, fetching outdoor clothes preparatory to an immediate departure for the clinic. One might speculate, as indeed I did, why the younger members of this family appeared so patently normal in the face of Kim's deepseated disturbance.

I will try to show some of the factors which contributed in the early stages to undermine the security of the mother–child relationship (so that the balance had swung heavily on the negative aspects), until both mother and son found themselves in that frightening situation of their love-ties being lost in a sea of resentment and frustration which at times amounted to murderous hatred. Melanie Klein's work with infants and young children demonstrates that deprivation increases greed and persecutory anxiety. In *Envy and Gratitude* she observes that when the relation to the good object is seriously disturbed not only are inner security and peace interfered with but character deterioration sets in. 'For to persecution are added the guilt feelings that the persecutory internal objects are the result of the individual's own envious and destructive impulses. . . .' Earlier work of Freud illustrated that individual variations in development were often due to constitutional factors and Melanie Klein substantiates this view. 'I have had many opportunities in my analytic work', she writes, 'to trace the origin of character formation to variations in innate factors', adding, as I had reason to recollect in this case, that infinitely much more needs to be understood concerning prenatal influences.

Allowing then for the differences of innate endowment in the three children of this family, I soon learnt that Kim's early history was not very heartening. The pregnancy was unplanned, unwanted and fraught with fear and apprehension, as will be seen in discussing the mother's background. 'I don't blossom in pregnancy', she announced ruefully. She 'threatened' a miscarriage. The birth was 'horrible' and feeding the infant 'a continuous nightmare'. At four months she virtually gave up and went back to teaching. Anna, a buxom country girl, was engaged as a mother's help and she took the thin, puling Kim under her ample wing and nourished him lovingly until her abrupt dismissal, on account of her own pregnancy, shortly before Kim's second birthday. It is a sad fact that, at times, the efforts of parents to spare their children the experiences of pain and loss merely serve to intensify a child's suffering. Kim was not told of Anna's departure nor was her name ever mentioned again. As a result he wandered about the house clutching a treasured piece of rag, he would not eat, became listless and apathetic and finally reverted to soiling. This small toddler showed all the symptoms of grief and mourning. In trying to understand Kim's development, it seemed likely that this sudden loss of a loved object revived earlier memories when the young baby feels he has destroyed his mother by his destructive impulses. Thirty years ago Susan Isaacs found 'that the child's earliest experiences of painful external and internal stimuli provide a basis for phantasies about hostile objects', and in more recent years Melanie Klein states that in the first few months of its life the child goes through paranoid anxieties related to the bad denying breasts which are felt as external and internal persecutors. It appeared possible that Kim's early feeding difficulties and the disappearance of a happy and close contact, at best, could serve to threaten his inner security and trust – at worst, could set a pattern of paranoid guilt that would influence his developing personality.

In assessing the present situation I was encouraged by the contentment of the younger children, and this mother's wish for help in her deep distress at the unwelcome feelings aroused by Kim's defiant behaviour and dispirited lack of educational prowess. The latter symptom was particularly painful to these parents when Kim's I.Q. was confirmed at 150+!

Following the diagnostic consultation, Kim's father came to see me and it was clear that this brilliant young man, with several degrees to his name, had, to a large extent, compensated for the loss of a leg at an early age by intellectual achievement. Feeling angry and bewildered about his eldest son, he continued to place undue emphasis on educational attainment, and had told Kim in no uncertain terms that should he fail to reach grammar school he would have nothing further to do with him. The breach between father and son was indeed formidable and I began to ask myself just who in this family would relinquish their heavily defended positions, if ever.

I have since wondered if it was David's evident pleasure in accompanying his mother to see me that aroused Kim's curiosity – or animosity. About two months had elapsed when Kim casually announced to his mother his intention of climbing a large pear tree in the clinic garden – tree climbing being an obsessional pursuit of his as I was soon to discover. This new element was discussed with the clinic team and I was given *carte blanche* by the psychiatrist – which wasn't exactly welcome as I could not imagine what I was going to do with this persecuted little boy. However, I offered to see Kim after school at weekly intervals, to which he silently assented. Thus for fourteen long weeks he arrived promptly, acknowledged my greeting with a non-committal nod and proceeded to climb the two pear trees with the ease and agility of a monkey – a mute monkey! Not one word did he address to me during these fourteen tree sessions, although I came to realize that he was communicating with me in other ways. I should point out that he would, of course, answer politely any question I might put to him, but I soon realized that this was valueless and confined myself to comments when I felt them applicable. I had noticed that despite his apparent concentration on every foothold, his eyes watched me covertly, much as one might keep a dangerous animal within one's sights. Imperceptibly this changed to the merest flicker of pride or satisfaction in that I continued to watch his every movement with interest – in fact it was so imperceptible that I could have imagined it, but I had nothing to go on except my intuition of this silent child. Gradually his field of garden activity widened and he began to make elaborate schemes with the rope ladder and other climbing equipment with an occasional word of encouragement or suggestion from me. At times he would disappear to the topmost branches where only the slight trembling of the leaves betrayed his presence. As week succeeded week with the same obsessional routine I literally began to dread this hour and to feel depressed, bored and angry. Doubtless many therapists would have successfully interpreted his behaviour, but I required at this point to review my feelings of frustration and inadequacy because my 'food' was being rejected. Nevertheless he came with unfailing regularity although it seemed a very long testing-out period. At the end of the fifteenth session he uttered his first voluntary remark, 'See you next week' he said as he went out of the door – never have four words come to assume such significance for me.

Nature came to my aid as the evenings were drawing in and I mentioned that it would soon be too dark to climb out of doors, so I wondered aloud if he would like to paint or use any of the other materials in the playroom. In spite of his polite agreement, he continued the tree climbing with a renewed urgency that revealed his anxiety. The day came when he met me with a jumbled incoherent sentence from which I sensed rather than heard that he would like to try the poster colours. None of us in the clinic were quite prepared for the black despair that emerged in Kim's first paintings. I still have these original drawings which would surely qualify for the most primitive of witch doctors' masks, used to ward off evil spirits. He outlined

two leering faces from whose ears and mouths ballooned pro-
hibitory messages – NO SMOKING, CLOSED FOR LUNCH,
KEEP OUT, DANGER, NO FIRES ALLOWED, SILENCE.
It will be remembered that Kim's surname was the same as our
psychiatrist, Dr A, so it was interesting to note that these paintings
were labelled respectively Dr A and Mrs Dr A. We were agreed
that of the two, Mrs Dr A was by far the most diabolic representation of the 'witch mother' that we had seen in a long time. It was
remarked that some release might follow this upsurge of unconscious material but I was agreeably surprised at its swiftness.
The following week his mother reported that Kim's teacher had
asked her if anything unusual had happened with him as he had
suddenly produced a spurt of careful and well-directed work
which had warranted individual praise both from herself and from
the headmaster. This was particularly evident in historical essays,
his store of knowledge surprising everyone, including himself.

The painting sessions continued with increasing fervour in
comparative silence, but by now it was a companionable hour and
Kim had serious work in hand as I observed his growing reluctance to stop at the appointed time. In spite of his phenomenal out-
put as sheet after sheet greedily licked up the now brightening
colours, he kept a wary eye on me and I would often communicate with him by painting his name in a variety of designs which
sometimes produced a secretive half-smile. In time his devils began to take less frightening expressions and assumed a somewhat
wry, humorous demeanour as if apologizing for their horns.
Casually I murmured something about finger painting and he
needed no second invitation. Scooping out great gobs of solid
brown paint I saw real pleasure in his face for the first time as he
named this masterpiece Dr Kildare A. 'Dare you kill him?' I
asked. With a wicked look that reminded me of his small brother
he filled a watering can and with the entire contents of the sand
tray he obliterated Dr Kildare, creating the most unholy mess I am
convinced he had ever been allowed to enjoy.

In previous months I had been unable to prevent further pressure being applied to Kim in the form of extra coaching and Mrs
Kim was telling me that the tutor had remarked on his lack of
conversation. With this in mind she had asked Kim whom did he
find it easiest to talk to. Without a moment's hesitation he gave

my name, which surprised his mother, as indeed it would have astonished me. 'What do you talk about?' she inquired. 'Oh, school and football, and history and things!' he replied, 'and do you know, Mummy?' he went on, 'she even knows when I'm bored and changes the subject!' So he had been getting bored up the tree and I had changed the subject to painting! I should dearly like to know what I said in those long conversations.

Kim's pictures changed from devils to pirates and then to galleons and Viking ships which he painted with remarkable accuracy. He flooded the room several times when we could have done with one of his ships to sail out of it. At last he felt safe enough to turn his aggression directly on to me. Knocking over the jar of cloudy paint water – accidentally on purpose as it were – he darted a quick look of apprehension at me, which I returned with a playful flick of water from my brush. Sanction given and received, he rapidly marshalled his ammunition and attacked me with paint and water until it looked as if I had become the incarnation of all his devils. I declare he even laughed silently, but his eyes danced with excitement whilst, wet and bespattered, I remembered the pale, withdrawn child that had stood in the same playroom seven months previously.

The water battles began in earnest after this, which was not surprising when I recalled that Kim had not been dry at the age of six. He had eventually been subjected to electric contrivances which effectively 'cured' him in a week. Needless to say water pistols became a source of great satisfaction to him and the visit of a group of students to the clinic was enlivened on one occasion by the unexpected sight of the psychiatric social worker, resplendent in floral bathing cap, being chased unceremoniously up the stairs by jets of water followed by one small boy in hot pursuit. It seemed that he was acting out his aggression towards his mother, and although I was concerned about my lack of interpretations I was reminded of Michael Fordham's view that much treatment of children is indefinite in the sense that nothing need be done of a direct character – 'if a child plays something happens which is therapeutic in itself', he notes. After nine weeks of water play I decided to trust my intuition to 'change the subject'. I asked him if he would like to see our workshop and his immediate and pleasurable response confirmed my instinct that he was ready

for something more constructive – to make reparation perhaps?
There followed a period of harmonious activity for us both, the
now blissful silence broken only by the sound of sawing or ham-
mering as he laboured to build a garden seat 'for the family'. This
state of affairs was rudely shattered when I 'forgot' to warn him
of my impending holiday. As I had noticed the lively, warm ex-
pressiveness of Kim's eyes in recent sessions, I suspect that I
could not bear to extinguish their lustre. For this is just what
happened when I told him I would be away for five weeks – his
eyes became dull and apathetic and he wandered aimlessly round
the workshop, a picture of stunned incredulity. It dawned on me
that this was how he might have looked as a two-year-old when
Anna disappeared. Was this the relationship that Kim and I had
revived which would explain the feeling of unity he had been able
to establish with me? Melanie Klein says 'at best such an understanding needs no words to express it, which demonstrates its
derivation from the earliest closeness with the mother in the pre-
verbal stage'. I recollected that much of Kim's communication
with me had been with his eyes as I imagine his eyes had followed
the devoted Anna in his babyhood.

In my ignorance and anxiety I attempted to compensate for my
blunder by bribing Kim with a birthday gift which he accepted in
scornful silence, disdaining to turn up for his first session after
my leave. Fortunately for us both, reprisal action was soon forthcoming. He marched purposefully into the playroom the next
week announcing clearly that we were going to have a real battle.
The moment of truth came when, filling a tin waste-paper basket
brimful of water, he turned me into a human waterfall – this time
I had no bathing cap for protection. My guilt expiated, we re-
paired to the workshop where he made three boats of balsa wood
and took them home.

During this time Mrs Kim continued to make considerable
progress in her self-imposed task of looking within herself. I began to see, too, why Kim had needed those silent and solitary tree
sessions, for his mother was an indefatigable talker and organizer.
The only child of elderly parents, Mrs Kim calmly informed me
that she had been told that her birth had caused total blindness in
her mother. She recalled the first time, at the age of four, when she
had guided her mother to the village shops, and how persecuted

he had felt with all eyes staring at them. I had noticed that when she was talking to me Mrs Kim would keep her eyelids closed for considerable periods and I wondered if as a child she had tried to 'feel' her mother's sightlessness. She had undoubtedly undertaken exceptional responsibility for her mother far beyond her years. As she grew older she realized that her father sought a series of extramarital relationships in the neighbourhood. This troubled her greatly when she could 'see' the evidence of these meetings and her mother could not. She linked this with her remorse about the times when she would make grotesque faces or stick out her tongue at her unsuspecting mother.

The tendency of parents to work out their emotional problems through the children is well known, and it gradually emerged that Kim carried his mother's unconscious guilt about her parents. As Mrs Kim grew able to comprehend her own feelings of hate and resentment so could she tolerate the manifestations of these in her first-born. She had been desperately afraid that Kim's birth would result in her own blindness or that the baby's eyes would be damaged. The subsequent births had not aroused these fears, possibly because by then all the badness had become focused on Kim, who obligingly filled the unconscious role assigned to him.

I had occasion to observe the child's intuitive understanding of his mother's feelings when Mrs Kim's ambivalent attitude towards her parents aroused acute anxiety at one stage. This was reflected in the small David, who insisted tearfully that he didn't like the sand any more and, seeking the comfort of his mother's lap, he sucked his thumb, looking reproachfully at me with his brown button eyes.

With her developing insight, Mrs Kim could withdraw many of her projections from her eldest son and she began to contemplate her relationship with her husband. She voiced her uneasiness about their sexual relations as she had consistently refused him since David's birth. She discussed her deep hostility towards her father's unfaithfulness and its possible relation to her husband's one lapse. This had occurred during their engagement when he had confessed to being responsible for another girl's pregnancy. Mrs Kim had dealt with this much as a mother might protect her son from an unsuitable entanglement, even supplying money for the confinement. Denying her anger and humiliation at the time she had stored it up over the years until it found an outlet in their present estrangement. It said much for this rigid woman that she could take the first step towards a reconciliation and a more equal partnership instead of treating her husband like another child.

Gradually, much of the strident unhappiness within the family abated, largely due, I believe, to the mother's capacity for change. Her determined appeal for help and her sincere and genuine pleasure in *both* her sons' relationships with me was remarkable for she never at any time gave evidence of the jealousy which often arises when two members of a family are seen regularly by one person in a clinic. Above all she had the courage to see what she had done and was doing to Kim. This painful realization reduced her verbosity to a silence deeper and more pregnant than any I had experienced with Kim. When her youngest goes to school Mrs Kim hopes to take a course in the teaching of maladjusted children, and I am certain that her skill and knowledge will be greatly enriched by the understanding of her own maladjusted son.

Mr Kim began sending friendly messages via his wife. Both these parents were highly ambitious and it was easy to see how Kim was expected to fulfil some of these driving forces. Mr Kim intent on seeking a higher post, wondered if I had any knowledge of such business matters, a request which somewhat nonplussed me as I pondered what it was he was really asking. However, I took it exactly as it had been conveyed to me and I made a point of finding out as much as I could concerning professional boards for managerial posts. Three months later Mrs Kim came looking pleased and happy, and, I thought, visibly softer. She was full of new plans as her husband had been selected for a much coveted and responsible post in a northern town. The whole family were eagerly looking forward to the move.

In the first instance no treatment plan could be made for this family, no social diagnosis attempted, but we tried to meet their needs as and how it was asked for, because we believe in the inviolable right of every individual to accept or refuse our kind of aid if they so wish. I have no desire to embark on child therapy but as a social worker this unusual contact with a child is an experience I shall always value. Without the support and interpretations of the clinic team I could never have withstood those silent hours.

At our last session he made a farewell sortie up that well-remembered pear tree. Scrambling expertly up the rope ladder he swung into the branches like a miniature Tarzan, exhorting me with a curious mixture of contempt and confidence to follow him. I really tried to scale the ladder but failed lamentably. His supremacy acknowledged, experienced and shared, he seemed to savour his triumph for a few moments before descending for one last wild chase round the garden with the water pistols.

We didn't say good-bye – at least not in words.

Life for Kim will not be easy. There are severe handicaps for him, not least of these being his unwillingness to accept analytic therapy for, as Kleinian child analysis has shown, it is through tracing back certain aspects of character formation to the early processes that changes in character and personality can be effected. I suspect that from time to time he will carry an outsize chip on his shoulder to disguise his vulnerability and painful insecurities. There is a story told of St Dunstan, that from time to time when he was preaching his disciples saw, to their horror, the Devil standing beside him. He simply turned and said 'Hello, are you there again?' and drawing strength from the association, calmly continued his discourse. I hope that like St Dunstan he will recollect the half-humorous devils he finally painted and come to know them, instead of treating them, and the world, as his deadly enemies.

Robina Prestage trained as a psychiatric social worker in 1958 and for eight years worked in Local Authority Child Guidance Clinics. She is now a supervisor in the St Charles' Group Hospital Management Committee's Child Guidance Training Centre in London for students from the London School of Economics who are taking a postgraduate course in Social Work. She has published papers on the theme of Separation Anxiety and in 1971 she toured Norway lecturing on the subject.

I I

Siblings of the retarded
1. Individual counselling

Children, vol. 12, no. 6, November/December 1965

Jane O'Neill

*This article and the next, no. 12, by M. Schreiber and M. F. Feeley, deal
with the needs of normal children with mentally retarded siblings. They are
included because, if little is written about children with overt problems,
even less comment is made about normal children in stressful situations.
How are they affected? Is mental handicap less acceptable than physical
handicap? Normal children have mixed-up feelings, sometimes protective,
sometimes hostile, about the handicapped member of the family. Parents
may not have the energy or perception to recognize the tensions or may even
wish to deny their existence. Social work intervention, where appropriate,
provides opportunities for the ventilation of feelings and for increased
understanding of the handicap itself.*

When a social worker is involved with the family of a mentally
retarded child, he needs to maintain a continuing awareness of
each of the other children in the home not only in order to learn
more about intrafamily relations and their effects on the handicapped child and his parents, but also for the sake of these children themselves. If the normal children in the family have problems
deriving from the presence of the handicapped child, the strain on
the entire family may be aggravated.

Sometimes the social worker derives adequate knowledge
about the other children in the family from the parents alone.
However, the worker may enlarge his understanding of the family
and perhaps modify his approach if he comes to know these
children personally. This usually contributes to a greater sense of
warmth and security all around, although some parents may feel
threatened by the agency's contacts with other members of the

amily, a possibility which has to be considered in the plan for ervice.

Getting to know the handicapped child's siblings may be chieved by plan or by incidental meeting. At the Evaluation and Counseling Program for Retarded Children in New Haven, we have found that the informality of our office often encourages parents to bring in the entire family when they come for an appointment. In fact, if parents come from a distance they sometimes turn the trip into a family excursion, climaxed by a treat, and we encourage this. Many of these families have experienced rejection and misunderstanding in the past. We try to make them feel accepted and at ease so that we can be of help to them in facing their problems. It might seem that the presence of several children for an hour or two in our small quarters could be disruptive. It sometimes is, but we find that we gain from each of these experiences both insight into specific family relationships and knowledge about the reactions of normal children to having a retarded brother or sister.

Out of such experiences grew our realization of the special problems faced by these normal children and of the help the agency could offer them. This, of course, varies with each child.

All that one nine-year-old boy needed to dispel his fears was to visit the office, see what went on in every corner of it, and meet the staff. He knew that his brother, a hyperactive child who was frequently in trouble, was undergoing evaluation, and he had reacted to this with symptoms of anxiety. At school he had been unable to concentrate. Assurances from his parents that nothing bad would happen to his brother had not helped him; but as soon as he entered the agency office on a visit with his parents his strained expression eased. Later, his mother reported that although he seemed less anxious after the visit, he was further relieved when the evaluation was entirely completed. He continues to be a very quiet boy who seems prone to worry, but, according to information from the school, he is participating normally in the classroom.

The question of whether older children should be included in family–staff conferences regarding a handicapped child is one which the parents must decide. The social worker can, however, help them make their decision. Various degrees of protective and

dependent feelings, and sometimes sound understanding of wha
each child needs and can take, will enter into the parents' decision
What the conference is to be about will also enter in. If, for in
stance, this is to be the first interpretation of the diagnosti
findings on the handicapped child, the parents may very well fee
that they should come by themselves.

This leaves still to be handled the problem of interpreting th
diagnosis to the other children. Usually parents will expect to d
this themselves. In most instances, by the time they have come t
the agency they have already established their own pattern fo
meeting children's questions, spoken or unspoken, about the de
fect, slow development, or strange behaviour of a brother or
sister. They are most likely to continue to follow the same patter
to a large extent, although they may modify it in the course o
their experience with the agency.

Even so, the parents may seek continuing or intermittent hel
with intrafamily relations. Such help may be given to them directl
or in some other way. There are times, for example, when th
parents will seek the worker's help in talking with an older chil
about a situation which has become very complex, which the
feel they have been unable to interpret adequately or satisfactoril
or which has especially upset the child. Sometimes the child him
self will signal his needs and a friendly conversation in the agency'
playroom will lead into something more purposeful.

One eight-year-old girl, frankly acknowledged by her mother a
'my right arm', was unable to remain away on any occasion whe
the parents brought her atypical younger sister to the office durin
an extended period of evaluation. She would at first express re
gret about missing play with her friends, but would then adm
that she had insisted on coming because otherwise she woul
have felt anxious. She said she always liked to know what wa
going on. She did not, however, show interest in observing an
of the evaluation procedures. This child had a need to talk, an
she showed that she thoroughly enjoyed and felt important in he
role as second mother to the retarded child. She said she wishe
her mother would have another baby. Then she said that sh
enjoyed those aspects of her sister's condition which made her co
tinue to be a kind of baby. She told of extremely conflicting fee
ings. On the one hand, the thing she wanted most of all was for he

sister to 'get better'. On the other hand, she wondered what it would be like not to have a baby in the house after being used to one for so long. She said she thought about this problem every once in a while.

The child's parents had tried to explain to her that her sister was not going to get better suddenly or dramatically. In talking with her, the social worker reinforced what the parents had said. Unfortunately, there was much about her sister's condition that was diagnostically baffling. The parents had been reacting to conflicting professional opinion and had not been able to keep their rising and falling hopes from the older child.

In the course of time, this little girl has seemed gradually to accept the fact that great change in her sister's condition is neither to be hoped for nor feared. She spends less time at home now. Her mother feels less guilty and depends upon other sources for help.

In other instances, we have felt it necessary to offer more formal and prolonged casework service to a sister or brother of a patient. There was, for example, Anne.

Anne was twelve years old when her parents asked for evaluation of her five-year-old brother, Freddy, a severely retarded, spastic child who was hyperactive and extremely difficult to control. To an increasing extent the life of all members of the family was being geared to Freddy's needs. Freddy had been on the waiting list for admission to one of the state training schools for about four years. However, the parents were not sure that this was what they really wanted. They had sought an evaluation of Freddy by the agency to help them make a decision and be prepared if the opportunity for admission occurred. The worker's first impression was that this was a very close family. All members, including Freddy, had a generally pleasing appearance. The mother looked careworn, but was very bright and controlled. The father, a clerical worker, was affable and mild in manner. He was extraordinarily patient with Freddy. Anne was pretty, serious, and even sombre. Later it was discovered that she was capable of great animation. Her eight-year-old brother, George, had a ready smile.

Anne seemed to feel a great deal of responsibility for Freddy. The mother said that when Freddy wanted to be comforted he would go to Anne; when he wanted to play, he went to George.

The parents were direct in their discussion of Freddy, but they tended to deny their own deep feelings about him. While they accepted the offer of continuing service from the public health nursing consultant, they made only limited use of the agency's help. By the time of the staff-interpretation conference, they had about settled on residential care as the ultimate plan for the child.

In spite of their independence in planning for Freddy, these parents admitted a sense of inadequacy in regard to Anne. They said they knew that she was deeply concerned about the home situation, but that she would not talk to them about this. They eagerly accepted the offer of an opportunity for Anne to talk alone with the worker, and Anne also responded positively. The social worker had four interviews with Anne. The girl used them primarily to ventilate her feelings. These related to her sense of being repressed at home, to her relations with each of her parents, to George and Freddy, and to friends at school.

Anne announced from the start that she had accepted the fact that the plan for Freddy was to go to training school. She seemed to look forward to it as possibly providing some relief and relaxation of the tension at home. Her understanding was that they would be able to bring Freddy home for visits frequently.

Anne expressed a sense of rivalry with her mother. She was convinced that she understood Freddy and that when her mother was not there to interfere she managed him well. She felt that he could be taught to do more for himself but that her mother lacked the patience for this. For instance, Freddy had not learned to wash his hands because if he dropped the soap he would have a tantrum and refuse to try again. Anne thought that he could be helped to learn by repetition, and she told of an instance in which he had, but this kind of procedure was very frustrating to her mother.

Anne said she thought that one possible advantage of the training school would be that Freddy would be taught how to develop his potential. She used part of one interview to ask about learning processes, and told of how she was able to apply some principles of child development she had learned in school. When asked if she thought her mother might be interested in knowing about these principles, Anne seemed to shrink. She said her mother would not converse with her on that level; that her mother regarded her as only another child. Anne felt that she was different from her mother, stronger in that she did not talk about her troubles – 'I'm more like Daddy.' At the same time, she recognized that things were hardest of all for her mother because she was in the house all the time. She was pleased when her mother joined a sewing club.

Anne said she knew she was considered to be a serious person, but that this was only at home – 'Outside I'm like everyone else.' She expressed ambivalence about George and commented that he had a good understanding of Freddy, 'More than I did at his age', and that 'this probably will mature him mentally'. She was frankly envious of George's ability to enjoy his own life to the full and of his imperviousness to scoldings. George and Freddy would fight, and this distressed Anne. Their behaviour interfered with her homework and for a while she was getting up at 5 o'clock every morning to study French.

Anne found real satisfaction in her relations with Freddy and in his response to her. She delighted in talking about him, and about what he liked to play. She liked to provide him with new experiences. One spring day she let him splash in the mud and she thought this did something for him. Her mother, who has very high standards of neatness, was upset.

Although she could see weaknesses in her parents and felt that in many ways she could do better, Anne was not entirely uncomfortable in her role in the family and in the protective structure which her parents had placed about all their lives. Although many of her observations and reflections showed capacity for independent thought, many of her concepts and values, and even expressions, reflected those of her parents.

An acute problem for Anne related to community attitudes toward Freddy. She found it hard to tell people about him and was especially afraid of telling her schoolmates. About two years previously, the family had moved to a suburb from the city. She found herself a newcomer in a school in which most of the children were from families of higher economic status than her own and, she thought, more secure socially than hers. There was one girl whom she admired very much. Once when retardation was

mentioned in school this girl said, 'But those children look awful.'
Nevertheless, Anne wanted to be liked by her. She held back from
social opportunities out of shyness but accepted an invitation to
the girl's home. She realized then that she was well accepted but
she continued to fear that this would change if the family problem
became known.

Anne thought that she would never have the courage to tell her
schoolmates about her brother's condition herself, and that she
would be considered deceitful if they learned about it in another
way. She and the worker discussed this problem at great length,
but Anne could not work out any entirely satisfactory plan for
handling it. She was pretty sure that not many people in the community knew about Freddy, although a few of her new friends
had seen him when they stopped at the home one evening to pick
her up for a party. When the worker asked what their reaction to
Freddy seemed to be, she said all they seemed to have seen was a
cute little boy. He had looked appealing at the moment. He had
just had his bath and was ready for bed. She was sure they had not
noticed anything. The girl about whom she was so concerned had
not been in the group.

Anne's closest friend was a girl from her old neighbourhood.
She knew all about Freddy and about Anne's problems concerning him. Fortunately, Anne had been able to continue in a close
relationship with this trusted friend.

When the worker asked Anne if she had ever had any experience of her own which would be useful to her in understanding
the reactions of others to Freddy, Anne recalled that many years
ago, before Freddy was born, a child who did not talk, visited the
family. She had not been aware then that there was anything else
wrong but now she knows he must have been retarded. She and
George played with him, and she remembers now that his parents
seemed very pleased. The worker asked how she thinks of this
person now. She closed her eyes and then said, 'Someone nice.'
She said she was afraid, however, that some people are prejudiced
against a retarded person before they even meet him.

At her third interview, Anne reported that her father had an
opportunity for a job transfer which would have some advantage
for him. It would mean moving out of the state. Her mother was
not in favour of it, on the grounds that the family might suffer a

financial loss in giving up the present home and acquiring a new one elsewhere, and also that the family needed to make sure of Freddy's continuing eligibility for admission to the training school for retarded children. Anne said, however, she thought the real reason her mother was against the transfer was that she did not want to move away from friends and familiar surroundings. Anne did not know what her father really wanted to do, but she felt that he must want a change because for eighteen years he had been working in close association with a person whom he 'couldn't stand'. This would be his last chance to change because he had declined a previous offer. Anne said she was feeling more and more puzzled at her father's way of giving in to everyone. She told about how he spent every Sunday driving two sets of relatives between their homes and her family's.

Anne was not quite certain what she preferred herself but she leaned toward the move. The problem of informing new friends about Freddy would come up again but perhaps she could make a different kind of start. She pointed out that although she knew about the question of the move and some of the circumstances related to it, she did not know just where her parents were in their thinking since they did not include her in making any decision of this kind.

At the next interview a few weeks later, Anne said that she did not know what the final decision about her father's job was or if it had yet been made, but she knew one thing was certain: whatever the family did and whatever happened in their house in regard to almost anything would be what her mother wanted. She seemed a little relieved by her own ability to recognize that this was a fact of her existence. She seemed less concerned about the home situation now and more about school. She groaned when she said that she sometimes felt that she would never get into college. The end of the school year was approaching, however, and she was looking forward very eagerly to a three-day trip to Washington with a group to which she belonged. At the end of this interview, Anne was not sure whether she needed to come to the agency again, so it was decided that the interviews would be terminated until she felt she wanted to resume them.

We have had no further direct communication with Anne. Her father was waiting as she left the office. In passing conversation, he revealed that the plan for job change had been definitely rejected.

A few months after this, Freddy was admitted to the training school. The mother reported that they had had to act on short notice and that perhaps this was good. She said she thought her husband was feeling the separation hardest of all. As for Anne, her mother said she seemed happier, 'a changed girl'.

Counselling service for the father was offered at this point but declined. The mother explained that she and her husband understood and valued the agency's interest but that they always felt that they should handle problems themselves as much as possible. She sent a message to the worker with the assurance, 'We're doing all right.'

Perhaps the agency might have given more help to this family, especially toward precipitating better communication among the members. The help which was provided, however, was in an area concerning which the parents recognized a need. It harmonized with the family's basic goals, although the parents' immediate goals were not identical.

For the girl, the agency's service provided an urgently needed outlet. In helping her, it released some of the tensions in the entire family. It also helped to increase the agency's own understanding of some of the problems faced in the homes of retarded children, the strengths which may be found in them, and the importance of giving them support.

Jane O'Neill is a graduate of Albertus Magnus College, New Haven, Connecticut, and of the National Catholic School of Social Service at the Catholic University of America, Washington, D.C. For nine years she was with a clinical service, the Evaluation and Counseling Program for Developmental Problems in Early Childhood. She is now a social worker with the Travellers Aid Society of Greater New Haven, Connecticut.

IV
Communicating in groups

Siblings of the retarded
2. A guided group experience

Children, vol. 12, no. 6, November/December 1965

Meyer Schreiber and *Mary Feeley*

In the course of providing group work services to retarded children during the past decade, the staff of the Association for the Help of Retarded Children in New York became impressed by the frequent references made by parents to problems these children created for their normal adolescent brothers and sisters, and vice versa. Parents expressed concern, for example, over the normal child's feelings of being overburdened by the care of the retarded sibling, of his overt expressions of hostility and resentment toward the retarded sibling, of responsibility for the retardation, of obligation to make up to the parents for what the mentally retarded brother or sister could not give them, and of guilt for being the normal child.

At the same time, the staff became impressed by the large number of normal adolescents who were taking their retarded brothers or sisters to social group meetings and to special events, and by other indications these young people gave of being able to cope with the fact of their sibling's retardation. Many of them obviously had been able to work out their feelings about their retarded brothers or sisters with no major intrapsychic, interpersonal, or intrafamilial strains, by developing healthy defences and using compensatory mechanisms.

Thus with evidence both of need and strength in the normal adolescent siblings of retarded children, the staff began considering what the agency could do to include such young people in its total efforts to strengthen family life in the families of retarded children.

Consequently, with agreement from the appropriate lay committee, composed in part of parents of the retarded and the agency's board of directors, the decision was made to establish a demonstration programme of guided group discussion for selected normal adolescents, through which they could examine, clarify, and understand more clearly a dynamic aspect of their life situation – their role as siblings of a retarded child. The experience in such a group, it was anticipated, would help these young people to become more effective and assured in their intrafamily relationships and responsibilities, and so would enrich the total family life.

More specifically, the aims of the demonstration were delineated as:

1. To assist the individual and the group to identify the nature of their reactions to having a mentally retarded brother or sister – stress, strain, mixtures of affection and antagonism – and the effects of these reactions upon their relationships with their parents, brothers and sisters, peers, and their entire life situation.
2. To help the individual and the group to examine and to clarify strategies for understanding and dealing with their siblings, their parents and peers, and the problems of daily living related to their status as the brother or sister of a retarded child – strategies which would be helpful not only to them but also to others in similar circumstances.
3. To throw light upon the extent to which the concern and reactions of such adolescents represent strength as well as intrapsychic, interpersonal, and intrafamilial strains, and to determine whether their defences are similar to or different from those of adolescents with no retarded siblings.

Since expressions of interest in the programme came from all parts of the city, it was decided to conduct the group sessions at the association's office, which was centrally located. To qualify for admission to the group, an adolescent had to be between thirteen and seventeen years of age, and be willing to participate in the group sessions every two weeks to discuss his problems and feelings in relation to his retarded brother or sister and his life situation.

Twenty-eight adolescents met these criteria. Obstacles to attendance, such as the day, time, and travel involved, reduced the number selected to participate to ten. Twenty other young people were interviewed by staff members and helped to see why they could not be included in the group. These included several who were 'pushed' by domineering parents to apply because 'this is good for you', others whose parents expected the group to provide a therapeutic experience, and a few whose needs were basically social. For many of these young people, the group experience might have been too anxiety-provoking or otherwise inappropriate. Unfortunately, shortage of staff members prevented follow up of those who seemed in need of individual counselling.

The ten young people who formed the group included five boys and five girls, mostly from lower-middle-class backgrounds. The age spread was from fourteen through seventeen, with the boys generally one to two years younger than the girls. Six of the participants were in junior high school and four in high school. Judging from their own comments about school, seven could be considered above average in academic ability and three as average students; and seven were involved in extracurricular activities at school. All participants indicated a real desire to participate in this new experience.

All the retarded siblings of these young people were living at home. Some were mildly, some moderately, and some severely retarded. Half were younger and half older than the normal brother or sister.

The group, which its members called the Brother-Sister Group, met every two weeks from October 1962 through May 1963, under the leadership of a professional group worker. The first session was devoted to a consideration of the voluntary nature of the group and what the group hoped to accomplish. The adolescents agreed on their own accord to come regularly, and to share their problems and experiences in order to help not only each other but also other teenagers in similar circumstances. At the end of each session the group agreed upon the focus of the next. In the beginning, the group worker took an active role in suggesting possible subjects for discussion, such as 'How do you tell your friends about your retarded brother or sister?' However, as the members became better acquainted and more comfortable with each other and the worker, they began to bring up spontaneously the concerns they wanted to talk about. These included such questions as: 'Does the fact that our family has a retarded member lessen our chances of marriage?' 'How can we deal with the feelings we get when our friends show us pictures of their brothers and sisters and brag about their accomplishments?' The participants offered little resistance to telling the group about their experiences with their brothers and sisters, families, and friends.

The worker helped the group look at different aspects of the material under discussion, adding information as needed, or raising questions and suggesting alternative courses of individual and group action. The worker also dealt with problems of individual needs and intragroup relationships. At the same time, she helped the group hold to its aims and special function. She filled a variety of 'roles' – confidant, leader, counsellor, resource person, agency representative, and even parent – as the situation demanded and the group progressed.

By the fifth session a cohesive group had emerged, held together by a common bond and meaningful relationships between the members and between members and group worker. From that point on, the group was largely self-directed, taking major responsibility for the content of the meetings and for individual participation. The group worker became largely a resource person, who provided clarification of points, support for individual participants, and information to indicate alternative courses of action.

Each session lasted an hour and a half, and included a period of light refreshments provided by the agency. At the end of each, the worker summarized the progress made, emphasizing the positive, the constructive, and the realistic aspects. She encouraged the members to share their findings with parents, other normal siblings in the family, and friends; and to feed back significant reactions from them to the group. Such reporting back was frequent.

The group usually stuck with an issue until it reached a termination point. Completion of a subject of discussion sometimes took as many as three sessions. The group worker's attitude of constant acceptance provided a safe climate for the expression of concern and the ventilation of feelings whether these were of hostility, hate, or love. The participants also found support and recognition of the right to be different from their peers. They learned a method of analysing life situations which was not only appropriate to the current scene but which could be used in dealing with future problems as well. Attendance at sessions over the eight-month period averaged 92 per cent.

What were some of the common problems which emerged? The following list was prepared by members and group worker together. The illustrative material comes from the group records.

1. How do you tell your friends about your retarded brother or sister, especially friends of the opposite sex?

At this point, Bonnie turned to Susan and said, 'Should I ask the question?' Both girls giggled, and Susan encouraged Bonnie to ask it. The question was: 'How do you tell a boy that you have a retarded sister?'

Mark responded immediately by telling about his experience in telling a girl about his sister. The girls listened attentively, but then Susan said, 'It's different telling someone that you really care about.'

Susan is 'going steady' and she hopes Stanley will never find out about her retarded sister, Gail. Could she tell why? She feels ashamed and embarrassed.

Kenneth said he knows how Susan feels, but he has been trying to help himself by asking whether he would be ashamed if his sister had no arm or no leg. He said knowing about this should have no effect on a person who had nothing to do with it, and if the boy really cares about you, this won't change him. Kenneth told us that a few weeks ago a girl asked about his sister and he did not tell the exact truth. He felt ashamed about the way he acted and made up his mind to tell the truth the next time he saw this girl, but he just couldn't get himself to do it. He knows that it was wrong but he couldn't help himself.

2. How do you deal with your parents who have not discussed the problems of mental retardation in the family and their implications for you?

3. How do you deal with friends and people in school when you are hurt by their talk of the retarded as nutty and crazy?

4. Are these meetings really helpful or are we betraying our families' confidences?

5. Are our parents' expectations concerning our role and their role in continued care of our brothers and sisters, real and fair to all involved?

6. What should be our responsibility toward our retarded brother or sister in the event of our parents' deaths?

Even before the meeting began the teenagers were discussing among themselves the requests made by their parents for the care of the retarded sibling if anything ever happened to the parents. Regina and Diane have promised never to send their retarded siblings to an institution. Bonnie promised to visit her sister Barbara regularly in the institution. She would definitely not care for her if her mother were unable to do so. The other girls laughed at this and told Bonnie that she was 'just talking' again, and that she would be the first one to object to having her sister placed in an institution.

7. What are we to do when our parents do not really feel affection for our retarded brother or sister?

8. How can we deal with our feelings when our friends show off their brothers' and sisters' pictures and talk about their accomplishments?

Bonnie broke in here and said: 'It is hard when you hear the other girls boasting how smart their sisters are, and the things they do, and you can't say anything about your sister. In fact, very often I do not admit that I have a sister at all. Some of the girls in school think I am an only child and others want to know if I have a brother or sister since I never talk about mine . . .'

9. Does retardation in our family lessen our chances of marriage, and is it hereditary?

10. How can our parents help us with our problems?

11. What can you do together with your retarded brother or sister in the home or in the community?

12. How does a teenager really accept a problem that he will face the rest of his life?

13. How can a teenager plan for his adult life?

14. What are our hopes for the future?

At this point Kenneth asked why Susan had such feelings about her sister. He thinks that they should all be very happy that they are living now when so much is being done for retarded children. Years ago people would hide retarded children and nothing was done for them.

Bonnie said that was easy to say but the fact remained that the situation was hard to face. She says that she has heard all these things before. You are supposed to feel good because the President of the United States, who is very smart, has a retarded sister.

Other feelings expressed by participants in the group were: a feeling of not being loved as much as the retarded child; jealousy, resentment, and hostility toward the retarded child; denial of the severity of the retarded child's condition; and guilt about having negative feelings toward the retarded child. Such feelings, however, were not characteristic of the group, and their intensity in the individuals who held them was often repressed. The worker recognized their significance but did not delve deeper or bring them into focus before the group in view of the anxiety that would be evoked. Rather, she held to the group's educational focus, leaving the resolution of deep and involved feelings as the function of individual therapy.

As part of the group's activity, the worker suggested, after about eighteen sessions, that the participants might want to consider ways and means of helping other young people who had a retarded brother or sister. This resulted in a group project, the writing of a pamphlet directed to other teenagers.[1]

OBSERVATIONS

Over the eight-month period, the experience with these young people led members of the agency staff to make a number of observations. We present them as hypotheses which need further testing with a larger number of retardates' siblings – young adults as well as adolescents.

About the normal adolescent

1. It was not the degree or kind of retardation in his sibling which seemed to affect the adolescent's life or happiness as much as

[1] Brother-Sister Groups, Association for the Help of Retarded Children, New York City Chapter, *It's tough to live with your retarded brother or sister*. New York, 1964.

the way he felt about himself and his retarded brother or sister, and the way in which he learned to live with the fact of having a retarded sibling.

2. What the normal adolescents really needed and wanted was accurate, up-to-date information, in language and concepts which they understood, about mental retardation and what they could do to help their families and their retarded siblings. They wanted to know how to manage *now* and what they could look forward to.

3. The young people's attitudes were not consistent at all times.

4. Almost every adolescent in the group brought up the question: '*Why* did it have to happen in my family, to us, to me?'

Kenneth said the question of 'Why did this have to happen to me?' comes to him often. I told him this was a natural question, but said I wondered what it meant in the way of his making friends, or in school. . . . He said that it hadn't meant much up to this point but wondered what would happen when he has to tell a girl about his sister. I pondered that question too. (He is unable to use the word 'retarded'.) He said he would just say his sister was different. He mused that everyone has something in their family. One of his friends doesn't have a father – parents are divorced. He can see this as a real problem. I asked him if this friend might also ask himself, 'Why did this have to happen to me?' and he admitted that this might be so.

5. The sessions helped the teenagers see some of the strengths, as well as limitations, in their brother's or sister's functioning, and in the family.

6. The importance of good communication and feeling between parents and adolescent depended on the existence of the kind of relationship which encouraged the adolescent to go to his parents whenever he felt the need.

7. The teenagers seemed to be helped by the very fact of knowing that the agency was interested in them as well as in their parents and their retarded siblings.

8. The group worker to be helpful had to look at life as far as possible through the adolescents' eyes, show her care and respect for them, and treat them with dignity and understanding. She had to be careful not to generalize and assume that the

problems and feelings of all the siblings of retarded children are the same.

9. The group worker found it important not to underestimate the strength of adolescents or to expect too little of them. It was clear that the young people wanted their parents to involve them in planning for the total family.

About the group and the group worker

1. The experience was appropriate for the adolescents in the group. They were able to express spontaneous feelings, to invest themselves in the experience, and to extract positive help and strength from their contacts with others who are in similar circumstances. For other adolescents such an experience may be anxiety-provoking to the point that the youngster is not able to handle his feelings appropriately. In some instances, such as when family relationships and parental roles were discussed, an adolescent's group experience carried a potential threat to his parents.

2. The meetings had meaning for the group not only in giving the young people help during a period of hardship, but also in helping them to maintain and build healthy family relationships.

3. The support of others – their peers and the worker – was helpful to these young people.

4. The size of the group was important. Ten members seemed about right for providing good opportunities for exchanging experiences and sharing the worker with each other.

5. Timing the meetings in relation to the many pressures on teenagers – school work, social life, family obligations, and work – was important.

CONCLUSIONS

Thus we concluded that this short-term group experience was useful to the teenagers involved. The spread of time helped the young people, at an age when it is difficult to put feelings into words, to open up problems, to delve into certain aspects of relationships, to pull together and integrate what had been accomplished, and to begin to think more realistically about the future.

The sessions did not always contribute to modification or change of basic attitudes, but they enabled the participants to know that others knew and experienced similar problems and that it was all right to feel the way they did. Although their problems and feelings could not always be resolved since some were 'bottled up' inside, for the most part these adolescents gradually became able to express their feelings more fully as meetings progressed and to become more realistic in their appraisal of them. This seemed to result in their being better prepared to see the next steps necessary in their planning. As time went on, they seemed to be able to look at the broader implications of mental retardation not only for themselves but for others who also had retarded brothers and sisters.

Many parents of retarded children are panicked into the belief that their retarded child will adversely affect his normal brothers and sisters. However, in some families where the parents have dealt with the situation constructively, such young people have developed greater maturity, tolerance, patience, and responsibility than is common among children of their age. Our experience suggests that the young person with positive family relationships is often capable of enduring the emotional hurt and anxiety of having a retarded sibling without severe disruption of his family and social life. He needs reassurance and support, but more often his primary requirements are educational. The more clearly normal siblings of the mentally retarded can see the realities of their particular situation, the better position they are in to cope with them. This is the point of a group experience.

As the young people wrote in their pamphlet:

We helped each other. We learned how to 'talk' about retardation and felt free to discuss our problems. We helped each other to be better prepared for any unexpected behaviour of our brothers and sisters. We knew that we were not alone.

Meyer Schreiber is Associate Professor of Social Work at Fordham University School of Social Service, New York. He has served as consultant to the United States Children's Bureau on social services to the mentally retarded. Currently he is involved in research and writing in the area of Social Policy and the Handicapped. He is Chairman of the

A guided group experience

National Association of Social Workers' Committee on Social Work and Mental Retardation.

A social worker in the New York City Department of Social Services for more than thirty years, Mary Feeley is now Director of its Community and Public Relations Program concerned with special services for children.

13
Group work with children
Ruth McKnight

Ruth McKnight offers for our consideration group work as a valuable resource for social workers. She does not believe in the random bringing together of people which sometimes occurs and which frequently results in disillusionment all round. With her colleagues, she has evolved from various group work theories and the realities of current practice, a method which has proved effective in facilitating communication with children of all ages. Anyone wishing to embark on group work will find this article full of helpful observations. The amount of work involved; the preliminary discussions among the staff; the careful selection of children; the home visits and the record keeping, apart from the management of the groups themselves, may deter the uncommitted. Others, extracting from the paper the immense contribution made towards the children's development and the therapeutic, social and educational benefits for them, will be stimulated to utilize this method of social work. But Mrs McKnight stresses the importance of being clear about goals and of advance planning. Training courses or involvement with groups run by experienced workers would be advantageous to anyone considering group work.

I have always felt that too many social workers concentrate too heavily on work with adults. It is as though they have forgotten in their 'grown-upness' how to communicate with children. Yet surely, so often when a social work agency becomes involved with a family, the children have already become damaged by their experiences and need direct work themselves to help them to come to terms with their feelings.

As a caseworker I do not, of course, dismiss a casework approach, but again how many of us forget that some, if not most, of the children and young people who need our help come from nonverbal backgrounds? At best, therefore, it can be a waste of time and at worst it can be a non-helpful process to put them behind a desk and expect them to talk.

Like any good doctor, we need as social workers a variety of tools to help such clients. I myself have used play therapy, for example, on the lines suggested by Virginia Axline in *Dibs in search of self*.

However, I have also found the use of groups for my younger clients increasingly helpful. Again, I feel we have to remember that many of the children and young people with whom we come into contact have missed out on family life, which should of course be the first, good, group experience. School has, on the whole, been a negative experience for them, and perhaps we are in a position to provide the first positive group experience in their lives.

Basically, I subscribe to the current teaching on group work and have found helpful such standard works as Bion[1] with his theories about roles, pairing, fight-flight and basic assumption groups, and Gisela Konopka's[2] book on the use of small groups. My feelings are perhaps best summed up, however, by Sarri and Galinsky[3] when they write:

> The goal of the social group work practitioner is the achievement of change in individuals who have social functioning problems, and the group serves as the means and context for the accomplishment of the desired changes. Because the group serves as the primary vehicle for change, it is viewed as a 'context' for treatment. The group as a 'means' for change, refers to the explicit use of group conditions to affect changes in individuals.

They also identify several valuable points for a social group worker, with which I agree, namely:

1. The Group is a potent influence system and can be used as an efficient vehicle for individual change.

---

[1] W. R. Bion, *Experience in Groups*, Tavistock, 1961.

[2] Gisela Konopka, *Social Groupwork – A Helping Process*, Prentice-Hall, 1963.

[3] Rosemay C. Sarri and Maeda J. Galinsky, 'A Conceptual Framework for Teaching Group Development in Social Groupwork', paper presented at the Annual Meeting of the Council on Social Work Education, Toronto, Ontario, January 1964.

2. The Group is not an end in itself, the aim of social group-work is to maximize the potentials of the group for individual change rather than to create a viable task-orientated group.

3. Group development can be controlled and influenced by the worker's actions.

4. There is no one optimal way in which groups develop.

The latter is a particularly significant assumption, because in much of the earlier groupwork literature it had been assumed that all groups must develop into democratic self-directing entities embellished with formalized operating and governing procedures. In contrast, we assert that pursuit of individual change goals for clients should direct the practitioner to intervene to affect group development in ways which facilitate the attainment of these particular goals.

Most of what I am about to say, therefore, is mainly in accordance with current group work theory, but it is also the result of my own and my colleagues' direct experiences of working with children in groups. My group work has been carried out in two agencies – probation and child care. In the probation setting I worked with common problem groups, such as girls just released from Borstal, and natural groups, such as a group of girls placed on probation together after a shop-lifting spree. In children's departments I have worked with groups of all ages, and mainly the children I and my colleagues have worked with have been living with their own families. We have also run purpose-made groups of children in a residential establishment, to assist children about to go out of care, for example, and we have also included children from foster homes from time to time.

Although our groups are purpose-made, and generally not open-ended, this does not imply an artificial composition. Either referrals to the department of children and young people in a particular age group and with particular needs have been numerous at some point in time, or children already under our supervision have displayed particular problems which lead the visiting officer to feel that some amongst them could be helped by a group experience.

Starting at the beginning, selection and composition of groups are important. From our experience, as far as numbers are concerned, we feel that the optimum seems to be between six and eight members and that a membership of lower than six does not allow sufficient interaction and development of roles and relationships, particularly if one or two do not turn up for a session. Working with more than eight makes a group unwieldy and leads to great practical problems of space and transport, let alone more profound difficulties connected with control, giving the children adequate attention, and other factors.

In any group it is advisable not to spread the age range too wide because of children's natural interests and activities. The age of the children affects the group's sex composition for the same reasons. Some boys of ten have strong objections to the thought of girls in their group. Fourteen- and fifteen-year-olds take quite a different attitude.

Still considering composition, we had to face the question 'From whose caseload?' Most current group work theory advocates, particularly in an office setting, that the group worker should not be the officer ordinarily visiting the child's family. We would tend to agree with this from our experiences as an ideal to aim for. But remembering the pressures on most social workers, we have also found that it is possible to work with children from an officer's own caseload. It is not advisable to mix children from the group worker's caseload with children from other people's caseloads. This tends to raise problems deriving from the relationships of member to worker which existed before the life of the group, and which are continuing for those children the group worker is dealing with outside the group. This makes it more difficult for the worker and the children, and confuses the issue when ongoing evaluations commence.

Given these factors we look carefully at all our possibles, assessing their individual problems and known and likely behaviour patterns so that we can select members, and formulate the overall aim of the group and its objectives. We have found that it is possible to select members whose difficulties dovetail in some way, such as common problems and difficulties in making peer group relationships, or children coming from single-parent families. We have also found it advisable to choose personalities which perhaps complement each other in some way, for example incorporating verbal and nonverbal children in the same group.

To achieve this we carry out a very definite exercise. From staff discussion groups it becomes clear that the problems are such with a number of children from a particular age range that a group for children of this age would be helpful. As a staff group we discuss this and the group leader is appointed, taking into account individual preferences about the age and sex of the children to be worked with, and, of course, work pressures. Often we use two workers in each group, sometimes using a student on placement with us as an assistant group leader. This helps when we try to give each child adequate attention, and makes for better observation on individual children. It also gives the child a choice of adult to relate to, and in many cases we have given a group a male and female worker – a mum and dad figure. The leaders have to be constantly alive to members' tendencies to try to play one off against the other.

Each officer who wishes someone from his caseload to participate in the group, writes a short social history outlining what they feel the child's problems are and how they feel the child can be helped by the group experience. The group leader, after consultation, then decides on the group's membership. Given these referrals from the officers, and the chosen membership, the leader then formulates specific aims and objectives which are immediately written down. For example, an aim might be to help the children through their feelings about parents and adults generally.

One thing we have found as the result of hard experience is that it is unwise to include an extremely disturbed child in a group. The inclusion of such a child too early, and too quickly, leads to him becoming the immediate scapegoat, which can be harmful for the child and the group. It takes a very great deal of skilled manœuvring to retrieve this situation. We tend to work with such a child by means of face-to-face play situations instead. When the child has worked through some of his problems we may transfer him to a group situation later.

If the leader takes from other officers' caseloads, parallel work is done by them with the child's family. There must be constant liaison, therefore, between the group worker and the officer for an interchange of information, though always being careful about confidentiality for the child's sake, even within the office. This liaison also helps when inevitably the child begins to try to play off the group worker against his officer. If a child tells me, as group worker, that he has a problem completely outside the group situation, I always advise a discussion with the child's own officer, explaining that they can do more about it. Or I ask if I can mention it to the officer. Sometimes the child is hesitant at first, but invariably agrees finally. If a problem from outside is impinging on the group situation, then I will deal with it and perhaps also ask permission to talk to the child's own officer.

Once the group has started there are all sorts of pressures to include other children. For people starting group work, I advise resistance to such pressures. It interrupts the developing life of the purpose-made group and confuses roles and evaluations. If, for some reason, I do allow an additional member, introduced by myself or some group member, I have always made it a matter for a full group discussion. Generally we have found that the children appreciate that there are limits imposed by premises and transport facilities and they like to feel exclusive.

We have not found it necessary to ensure that members of the group did not know one another before the group started. After an initial pairing or subgrouping we have found that as a group develops these subgroupings are more influenced by the whole group process.

Before a group actually gets under way we have made it our practice for the officer who ordinarily visits the family from which a prospective group member comes, to discuss his or her attendance in simple terms with both the child and the parents. If they are agreeable, and we have never had anyone refuse yet, the group leaders then go round to introduce themselves and discuss arrangements more fully. One of the sad things we have found is that very few parents care where their child goes, though when the child seems to be enjoying attendance at the group, the privilege of going is denied as a punishment. Even when the group is from our own caseload, we find preliminary visits of this kind helpful. It makes the group a special thing apart.

From my experience, I have found it essential to consult the children about days and timing, and it is also very important when dealing with children in groups to meet regularly, at weekly intervals, and as near as possible to the same time each week. This sort of built-in structure helps them. I know that even in the best-run agencies crises occur, but we have now made it a rule that if a crisis occurs for the group leader which would affect holding the group, then another officer deals with it or holds the situation. They would have to do this in any case if the group leader were on leave, ill or out of the office.

Having got this far, when I first started group work I had a great many fears and questions about what my role should be in the group. How could I control a group of children, they might get out of hand? How could I relate to so many at once, having only been trained in working with a one-to-one relationship? What should I do with the children and how communicate with them? These feelings were not really helped by the variety of literature at my disposal. Having read as much as I could these fears had to be overcome and dealt with in actual practice. Over the years I have learned some very valuable lessons.

My first lesson was in direct connection with my role. My experiences hitherto had been of discussion groups with a self-effacing sort of leader who was almost one of the group. The children, in fact, taught me that this was impossible in our setting and moreover it was not what they wanted. In an actual incident some teenagers clearly spelt this out.

We now feel as a result of our experiences that we have a role in a group which we cannot avoid, which is implicit in our official status and our agency. Theoretically this is best described by Kenneth Heap, a lecturer in social group work, at the Norges Communal Cosialskole, Oslo, in his article on 'The group worker as central person':

In casework the context of treatment is a one to one relationship in which the client is assured of the attention of the worker. The relationship between them is the main tool of the helping process. In social group work, however, there is of course a somewhat different orientation. In any group, certain group phenomena will be evidenced, such as initial exploratory and competitive behaviour, giving way later to mutual identification, cohesion, support and control. We accept these and other group processes as viable and sometimes powerful means of influence and help, and feel that the central skill of the social group worker lies in influencing and intervening in these group processes in order to mobilise and utilise them for the maturational or therapeutic task of the group. However, in putting great emphasis on the importance of helping group members through their relationships with each other, and we are not denying the importance of this, I sometimes feel that the relationship with the group worker as a source of help has been underemphasised in most work on social group work. Members do react to each other obviously, but they are all also at all times in contact with the worker, no matter how tenuously, and may only have a very sketchy contact with certain other members. Sometimes at the beginning of a group he may be the only person who has met them all, and in this sense may alone provide both focus and stability. Members are also aware at all times of the worker's initiative in forming the group. By our very existence, and that of our agency, we make possible their activity as a group. (*Case Conference*, vol. 12, 7 January 1966.)

Our role, therefore, is by no means a passive one. We do try to make positive relationships with every group member and to show ourselves in a definite role. Young children and teenagers find security in such a role, and I found that when I had come to such a decision about my role my questions and fears about control lessened, and the children responded to such an attitude.

Lesson number two, which I have mentioned before, was that with the children and young people who come into contact with us, it is no use aiming for a pseudoanalytical type 'T' group. These children come largely from nonverbal backgrounds. Thus, trying to run discussion groups as such with these children is asking for trouble. Older teenagers can take more pure discussion than younger children, but I have found that my most valuable talks, even with an older group, arose indirectly out of our activities. With children under thirteen years I do not even plan now for pure discussion. I aim for an activity group to promote discussion.

In general terms, with boys, say, of between eight and ten years, we have played football, gone on picnics, and gone to the zoo and the local airport. We have also been to the circus. I always include such excursions and games in a group programme and tend to intersperse outings with activities designed for the group room.

For these boys I have paints, Plasticine, jigsaws, comics and model-making kits. All these things can be used for unified group projects or for pairing or subgrouping situations, or they allow a certain amount of withdrawal for a solo effort. We have also raided office stock for dressing-up clothes.

With younger teenage girls, we have sewing kits, tapestry kits, jigsaws, books and cookery equipment, which they use in our office kitchen. For outings we have gone swimming, to the cinema and to the airport. With older girls I have gone ice-skating, swimming and to the cinema. Make-up and hairdressing sessions have proved popular, and cooking. Although on the surface these girls seem sophisticated, they have even enjoyed birthday parties with such things as jellies, at their own request, which shows how young they are inside.

Older children who are working tend to pay for their own outings. We have supplemented or paid outright for the younger ones. Some people have criticized us for taking the children on outings, but I feel strongly that these are children who miss out on most things in life. They are culturally as well as emotionally deprived, and lack social competence. Throughout, the group experience is progressing and the children are being helped by their relationships with each other and the leader.

Moreover, the programme using these activities is not haphazard, rather it is planned in a very definite way. In this respect we have found helpful the paper by Rosemary Sarri and Maeda Galinsky of the School of Social Work in the University of Michigan, to which I referred earlier. In it they attempt to break down the developmental stages in group process and they define the leader's role at each stage. The stages they outline are:

1. The origin phase
2. The formative phase
3. The intermediate phase
4. The revision phase
5. Intermediate stage two
6. The maturation phase
7. The termination phase

Writing about each of these phases they expound at length, identifying group members' behaviour clearly, and thus showing the worker what he should be looking for, and how to identify the phase. This goes from phase 1, which is the setting up of the group and preconditioning it for later development, to phase 7, the termination phase and the dissolution of the group.

Briefly, in phase 2, the formative phase, one sees the initial activity of group members seeking similarity of interests, a commitment to group purpose, and emergent interpersonal ties. In phase 3, the intermediate phase, the worker looks for a moderate level of group cohesion, and more established interpersonal bonds, amongst group members, clarification of purpose and observable involvement of members in goal-directed activities.

In phase 4, the revision phase, the worker expects a challenge to existing group structure and an accompanying modification of group purpose and operating procedures.

In phase 5, following the revision phase, the group generally manifests a higher level of integration and stability than in the first intermediate stage.

In phase 6, the maturation phase, one can see a certain stabilization of group structure and purpose, together with the existence of effective responses to internal and external stress, leading up to the dissolution of the group in phase 7, hopefully after a certain proportion of each member's needs have been met. In addition, in each stage, Sarri and Galinsky spell out the methods, both direct and indirect, which should be used by the leader to help individual members, and help work through the stages to maturation and termination. In other words, meaningful use of programme.

Having made his evaluation of what he hopes to achieve at the beginning of a group's life, our group leader then works out a programme, often together with group members. The programme is always governed by the forces at work in the group's particular stage of development, and is aimed at providing the experiences the worker feels are needed to help the group mature or achieve its therapeutic task generally, or to provide particular therapy for some group member.

An example of this, from an older teenage group, is that I planned for us all to go ice-skating. This was because one particular girl, Vivienne, had been made the scapegoat of this group, although she was unconsciously colluding in this role. In previous meetings she had given the impression of being retiring, self-effacing, and inferior, in all the group's activities. Fortunately, I discovered that she was a very good ice-skater. To discuss the fact that the group had made her the scapegoat would have been useless and inappropriate, but when the group saw her skating round the rink and performing various arabesques, something which they could not hope to achieve, they suddenly saw her in a new light. This improved the group's image of Vivienne, and helped her own self-image. These new attitudes were carried over into subsequent meetings, too. In the same way I used model-making to help a ten-year-old boy in a group.

To sum up, our programme is linked with the aim of the group, evaluation as to what is needed for group development, or a particular group member, and also natural interests of the children.

Diagnosis-wise we have found groups invaluable and I could quote numerous examples of this. I have been amazed, and impressed, at how the children handle each other's problems in a group. They knock the corners off each other and sort out an acceptable norm of behaviour. They help each other's communication problems and at the same time are sensitively aware of each other's difficulties. I have seen this in an older teenage group, where originally the members came from the 'unclubbables' for want of a better word. At the end of the group, six out of eight members felt able to go out and join more conventional youth clubs, something which they had been unable to do before.

Another example is with a younger teenage group. Twelve-year-old Beverley had been committed to our care and placed in a foster home. She was having a great conflict of loyalties between rejecting Mum and superb foster Mum. Suddenly Julia piped up, 'I bet you wish your Aunty Iris [foster mother] was your real Mum, Bev.' The group leader said afterwards that she held her breath, because she knew that Beverley's social worker had been treading gently on this point. But there followed a fascinating group discussion about ambivalent feelings towards mums, and as all the girls came from single-parent families they went on to discuss how it felt to be without dads. This was all of their own volition, whilst making decorations for the group's Christmas party.

Children also derive a great deal of help from their relationship with the group worker. On outings children have said to me, 'Miss, you do like going out with us, don't you?' I said I did. 'It is nice to have an adult to take you places,' said another. 'Miss,' said another, 'you really listen when we talk to you about school and things, and you remember our names and what we've told you.' At other times children have sidled up to me to tell me some snippets of home life and to get my sympathetic ear. One boy seemed to sum it up for the whole group when he said, 'Oh! Miss, we do look forward to Tuesdays, why can't we come every day?'

Another instance of help through the relationship with the worker was with a boys' group. I had missed a group session because of illness, and on my return the boys *en masse* decided to go into the country to play 'hide and seek'. The game consisted of me sitting in my car, my eyes covered whilst they hid. I then had to drive slowly after them and look for them. This was a very effective way of excluding me, and venting their hostility for my previous absence. Once, by accident, I did not see them, and drove past their hiding-place. Sense told me that they could not have gone as far as I had driven, so I turned the car round. I found a very anxious group of boys racing towards me. When they saw me there was a mixture of relief, joy and anger, summing up, 'We saw you go past, and we thought that you had left us.' So we sat down and I talked to them in simple terms about this. I said it was a mistake, but I realized that they had been upset because they thought I had gone without them. We talked about how horrid it is to be left, and to have grown-up support and interest taken away. I am sure from their attitude that each boy was relating this in some way to his own situation. I then went on to express that my absence last time could have made them feel this way, hurt and cross. At the end of our talk, the boys decided that they did not want to play hide and seek. They elected to return to the group room where they all desperately involved me in a painting project.

We have found that each group develops its own rules and traditions from within – 'because we've always done it, Miss'. In turn the leader, too, imposes some rules. Generally, with younger children, except when outings take place, we have set approximately an hour and a half's limit per group meeting. The children always want to extend it. With older children meetings tend to last two to three hours. We can set our own time limit, but we have to make it clear at the beginning of a group. If a child does not come for two sessions, I always visit because I feel it is harmful for a child to drop out.

Total duration of a group is important. It is possible to let a group work itself through all the developmental stages I mentioned earlier and in stage 7 the children will gradually drop out as their need for the group experience diminishes. It is also possible to set a limit at the beginning of, for example, three months or six weeks. Again, if we set such a limit, it is vital to tell the children at the beginning. Ideally, we like to let a group run its course. We have regular meetings as a staff group to discuss progress. We use Sarri and Galinsky's article and try to work out where we think the group is in its stage of development, and how we feel individual members are progressing. Then we go on to plan our own roles and the programme to help the group during this stage, or to help some individual member, as with Vivienne. A programme is then designed to help the group progress to the following stage.

Throughout its life, each group is recorded fully. The referrals of officers to the group leader and the aims worked out by the leader form the beginning of the group record. Each group meeting is written up, briefly outlining the group's activities and then each child's individual progress and reactions in the group. A final paragraph deals with the evaluation of the group's progress as a whole, and its stage of development.

Many people seem to feel that they cannot run a group because they lack ideal premises. We have run groups in the most unlikely buildings, including our own inadequate office. I am sure that a determined person could find something locally, for example a church hall, they could use. I know of groups that have operated successfully from a school playground during the school holidays. I also know of a very successful boys' group which used to meet weekly with a child care officer to go swimming, to go to a coffee bar, and outings generally. The child care officer's car was the only really fixed base they had.

Finance may be another problem, and transport, but again these obstacles are not insuperable. Even if official office funds are not forthcoming, I have found local firms very generous when approached for such a purpose.

I do most strongly advise social workers to try to help children and young people by this method. It is hard work, and I am not pretending that everything has always been straightforward. Children can be aggressive and difficult, and we have made mistakes. But speaking for myself and my colleagues, we feel that our efforts are well worth while. There is tremendous satisfaction to be gained from seeing how individual members, like Vivienne, develop in a group, and what adult social workers tend to forget is that working with children in this way is immensely enjoyable.

After gaining a degree in History from London University, a Diploma in Social Studies from the London School of Economics and a Certificate in Applied Social Studies from the University of Newcastle upon Tyne, Ruth McKnight worked as a Probation Officer in Sunderland and Stoke-on-Trent. She later became a senior Child Care Officer in Stoke-on-Trent. For five years she was Assistant Area Children's Officer in the Macclesfield Area Office of the Cheshire Children's Department. During this period, she lectured part-time at Keele University on the four-year combined degree/diploma Social Work Course. She was Senior Assistant for Personnel and Team Services in Cheshire Social Services Department before taking up her present appointment as Tutor in Charge of the part-time Residential Child Care Course at South Cheshire Central College of Further Education, Crewe.

14
Group work in probation

New Society, 21 February 1963

M K McCullough

Adolescent girls present an enormous challenge to social workers. Mary McCullough, an experienced probation officer, chooses group work to deepen relationships and to encourage real communication between herself and the adolescent girls for whom she is responsible. Despite the difficulties she first experienced in using this method, she values the opportunities it presents for verbal and nonverbal communication, for easing the conflicts that beset the clients and for offering a quicker way of learning more about them.

Both Miss McCullough and Mrs McKnight comment on the role of the group leader. The passive permissive role is too threatening, and therefore inhibiting, to children who expect positive leadership. The picture presented here of the typical seriously delinquent adolescent girl unable to make close relationships as a result of life experiences, surely indicates the importance of greater efforts being made with vulnerable children at a much earlier stage of their development.

In the treatment of delinquents there is no easy answer to the question of how to make contact. A probation officer may ignore the whole difficulty and proceed to deal with them by such methods of reasoning as commonsense and training suggest, counting on getting through to some of the clients some of the time, or, concerned by the shortcomings of this method, step off the well-trodden paths and experiment, even if this may mean floundering out of one's depth at times. It was on one of these forays, some years ago, that I first tried my hand at group work. I had heard a psychiatrist talk about his use of this technique in prisons and later had some opportunity to discuss its application to my particular field. I had also been daunted but not completely discouraged by reading accounts of the very much deeper, long-term work done in psychoanalytic groups. It is one of my duties to act as liaison officer to a probation hostel and I decided to start there.

Probation hostels receive young people between the ages of fifteen and twenty-one in whose cases a condition as to residence for not longer than twelve months has been made part of a probation or supervision order.[1] They are exposed to the influence and training of the staff, subject to fairly close supervision and expected to work regularly, avoid bad associations and so on. As may be imagined, a good relationship between hostel warden and probation officer is important if residents are to be helped and becomes more acutely so if anything more than routine work is to be done, particularly if it is to be attempted by group methods. Anyone who is the subject of a probation order may be sent to such a hostel but in the nature of things probationers so dealt with are likely to have more than usually severe behaviour problems or less than usually supportive homes, or both, and the following histories, selected at random, give some idea of the problems likely to be met and in particular of the paucity of close, continuing, meaningful relationships which is typical of the life experience of most seriously delinquent people.

Marion was illegitimate and, as often happens, was brought up as the youngest child of her mother's parents, regarding her grandmother as her mother. Grandfather was dead. She stayed with grandmother, two aunts and mother – whom she regarded as sisters, until she was six, when grandmother also died. Meanwhile, Marion's mother's immoral conduct had continued and soon after their mother's death her sisters quarrelled with her because of this way of life and she went away leaving the child in their care. The married sister moved to another district leaving Marion alone with one aunt, who worked to maintain them both, receiving a little money from the mother. She was not a very stable person

---

[1] Probation hostels are established with the approval of the Secretary of State under Section 46 of the Criminal Justice Act, 1948, with moneys provided by Parliament under Section 77 of that Act. They are managed on behalf of the Home Office by voluntary Managing Committees in accordance with statutory rules governing management. Since the coming into effect of the Children and Young Persons Act, 1969, they no longer accept anyone under the age of seventeen. Their responsibility is now for offenders between seventeen and thirty-five. – Editor.

and when Marion was fourteen she had a mental breakdown. Some months later, she became an in-patient and the child, after a short period with her married aunt, went to live with her mother. By this time she understood the facts of her birth. Mother had never married and shortly after Marion's arrival she became pregnant again.

The girl left school and would not work regularly. Just before her sixteenth birthday she was charged with stealing shoes from shops on two occasions and placed on probation. This was not a success – she would not work and was a determined liar and after six months she was brought back before the court and a condition of residence in the hostel was inserted in the order.

Bridget was the second of three children, born within a year or two of each other. While she was still a baby, father disappeared and mother began to live as a prostitute. Her father came home when the child was about two and found her and the other children alone in a room where there were many indications of their mother's irregular life. He informed the authorities, but appears to have taken little further interest in the matter and did not, in fact, see his daughter again until she was seventeen. What happened at the time is not clear but Bridget appears to have been removed from home for a short period and then returned to her mother.

When she was seven her parents obtained a legal separation and mother took the children to live with their grandmother, where they remained for the next six years, mother staying with them for part of the time only. At thirteen Bridget was sent to a children's home. Two years later, when she was old enough to start work, her mother came and took her away. There is no doubt that the mother was a woman of bad character and the man with whom she was then living was a convicted abortionist.

Two years later, then nearly seventeen, Bridget left her mother and went to live with a middle-aged foreigner. She left him after a short while and eventually went to a working-girls' hostel, where she stole some clothing. She was placed on probation with a condition of residence at the hostel.

Anne. Soon after Anne was conceived her father quarrelled with her mother and joined the Army as a regular soldier, serving abroad for long periods. Her mother lived with another man and a second child was born when Anne was two. Her infancy and early childhood were spent with her mother and mother's lover, whom she believed to be her father, together with her younger sister, in relative security.

When she was about five her real father returned. A total stranger to Anne, he took her away from his wife at once, to his parents in a different part of England. We can only guess what it meant to Anne when her whole world suddenly went to pieces, and at her fear and depression as, quite helpless, she 'settled down' in her new life. Not with the stranger-father – he returned to the army – but with his elderly parents.

When she was twelve there was some kind of family dispute, the origins of which are not clear. Grandmother wrote to her daughter-in-law and asked her to remove Anne at once. After she had been in her new home for three months her grandfather wrote and asked for her to be sent back. A few months later came the third great upheaval of her life. She was sent abroad to her soldier father and his new wife. She did not react to him with the daughterly respect and affection he expected – in fact twelve months later and about nine years after he had first taken her from her mother he wrote to say that unless her mother would have her back he would 'put her in a home'.

So just before her fourteenth birthday Anne came back to her mother. There was nothing equivocal about her reaction now. Wild, undisciplined, hostile and thieving, she went to the length of planting stolen articles on her little stepbrother and standing by while he was punished. Her mother said that after twelve months of Anne's behaviour she nearly had a nervous breakdown and I can well believe it.

At fifteen, she was sent back to her grandparents. She stayed out late at night and would not work regularly. A few months later she ran away and was found by the police who decided to bring her before the court as in need of care and protection. A supervision order was made with a condition of residence and she was sent to the hostel.

Theresa was born in Eire, some months after her father's death. She was a second child, the first having died, and her mother kept her until she was three and then placed her in a convent. Theresa told us that her mother never wrote to her, sent her presents or visited her, and this proved to be true.

When she was fifteen her mother sent for her to come to England. A year or so before this she had married a man much younger than herself. Later, in a group session this girl, who was normally uncommunicative, suddenly recalled this in bitter detail. 'I got off the train and there she was – she said she was my mother but I didn't know her, I thought to myself "She's not my mother, I hate the woman" – she was angry and said "What are you crying for?"' Theresa was taken home by this stranger to the one room which she shared with her new husband, where the girl slept behind a screen.

Within a few months she was hanging around a nearby army camp. She quarrelled with her mother constantly and absolutely refused to work regularly and to give her mother money, saying in the group later, 'I knew that was what she'd brought me over for.' One evening a policeman noticed her in Hyde Park with a coloured man. She gave a false name and age at first but later at the police station told them who she was and they sent for her mother. She left the station quietly with her, but once outside began to scream and cry and say that she would not go home. Mother said that she did not want anything more to do with her and she was brought before the court as in need of care and protection. A supervision order was made but Theresa's behaviour did not improve and a month later mother brought her before the court as beyond her control.[1] The original order was discharged and a fresh one made with a condition of residence at the hostel.

There is a growing amount of literature on the subject of group work and considerable divergence of aim and method, but there are certain basic requirements which are more or less common ground. It is generally considered that the group should consist of about seven or eight people. As few as five does not allow enough interrelationship to be significant and if there are as many as ten

[1] It is no longer possible for a parent to take this action directly. For current legislation see Section 1, Children and Young Persons Act, 1969. Editor.

or eleven it is difficult for the worker to hold each member constantly in her attention, and for the group members to relate continually with one another. Chairs are placed in a rough circle, preferably without a table, and people left free to choose where they sit, the worker's position alone remaining constant. This allows the members of the group to sit in whatever position they choose in relation to the leader and to one another and to adopt the posture which suits their mood and to change it as their reactions change. This nonverbal communication is significant, particularly so in my setting because delinquents for various reasons are not usually going to verbalize easily.

Selection of group members is considered of primary importance by some workers in this field: whether people should be similar, because then they will have more in common, or different because this simulates the real-life situation – or some particular combination of the two, like the Noah's Ark method by which two people are selected presenting each of several different problems, which allows each person to feel that they have something in common with at least one other in the group. For myself, I feel that human nature is so complex a thing that while I could match some characteristics – intelligence, for example, or the offence committed – I have no way of knowing whether these aspects of the total situation are the vitally important ones, and prefer to take my group members in the order they arrive at the hostel, which in effect produces a mixed group.

Then there is the question of how the purpose of the group is explained. With my groups I find it best to say very little, just that I think it sometimes helps them to talk over the problems they have in common. I give each girl the chance to refuse to come, although I only ever remember one doing so. The meetings last from an hour to an hour and a half and I begin to close them after an hour. I set a period to the group deliberately because in the delinquent authority situation people seem to tend to try to prolong a meeting which is due to close, whereas faced with an indefinite period of time they are more likely to resist with silence.

The groups meet weekly or biweekly on about six to ten occasions. This means in practice that a girl joins a group one to twelve weeks after her arrival at the hostel and stays in it for about three months. It will be appreciated that this is one of the critical times – the honeymoon period is over and people have not yet settled down. Before, during and after the group sessions I see the girls individually on an average of once every two weeks. My aim in the group is to deepen my relationship with the girls and to encourage real communication. The sort of group work that I do bears the same relation to group analysis that casework does to analysis – my aims are more limited and immediate and my interpretations rare and simple. I rely a great deal on the relief of tensions in the group, on the self-understanding which is achieved when the girl herself puts into words, perhaps for the first time in her life, something that she feels deeply and finds that these feelings are understood, and often shared, by others and also on the 'reflected' relief and understanding they sometimes get from hearing a fellow member express something they feel themselves.

At first I tried to achieve these ends by being the passive, silent enigmatic leader of the classical group-analytic situation. This puzzled and in a way frightened the girls who are used to me in a much more active role. I abandoned this attitude with reluctance only to find that the more I was willing to talk the less I was required to do so. My groups are now more or less leader-centred. In view of the total situation this would seem inevitable – and in fact has its advantages, because one of the ways in which the girls use the group is to come to terms with me as an authority figure, through this with authority generally, and so with their feelings about their parents.

In starting a session I make it clear that anything can be talked about and quite often they begin with a question – sometimes a very loaded one like 'Why are some girls sent to approved schools?'[1] If nothing comes spontaneously I attempt to stimulate, but not guide, discussion; that is, I aim to get them to talk about almost anything because, once started, they will reach with surprising speed something that is important to them – more often than not their troubles with their parents, however unconnected this may seem to be with the original subject. This is illustrated in the session described below. If, on the other hand, anti-

---

[1] As a result of the Children and Young Persons Act, 1969, approved schools are to be integrated into a system of community homes administered by Local Authorities.—Editor.

authority feelings are rife at the time, the discussion will lead to these. Incidentally, they seldom feel able to express direct hostility to me or to something I have done in so many words, but they can bring it out quite recognizably by talking about probation officers generally, or police or magistrates, or by nonverbal communications. If this happens I play the game by their rules and offer generalized answers and explanations.

What follows is taken from notes of an actual session, with names altered and identifying data removed. The girls in this session are necessarily not the same as those whose case histories are given above. It was the first meeting of a group of eight girls and I had already had two or three interviews with all but one of them. I began by greeting the newcomer, then explained the purpose of the group as simply as possible. They were quiet and unresponsive so, on the principle that when in doubt one should always take an obvious thing first, I asked them how they liked living together in a group. This also was received in silence, with signs of mild embarrassment and some giggling. I asked who had been away from home before and two or three volunteered brief information about periods in children's homes or boarding schools. Nearly all had been in the remand home. A discussion began on the relative merits of these institutions, swinging naturally to the question of discipline generally and then, gathering momentum, on to the subject of their parents. They supported the idea of discipline, which was generally identified with 'bashing', but some felt that they had been bashed too much and some not enough, and several said bitterly that they had not been bashed at all until recently which, didn't I agree, was too late?

This is a very two-edged question. On the face of it, I was being asked if adolescents are too old for corporal punishment and if I myself am going to bash or countenance bashing. This aspect of the question I answered with emphatic reassurance. But the underlying question must not be forgotten – they are asking, in a way, if it is 'too late' for them for discipline or anything else to do them any good and this anxiety about being in some way damaged or inferior came out more clearly later on, when they turned to the question of psychiatric examination.

Betty, the new girl, who had been sitting in tense silence, suddenly launched into an attack on her over-strict father and her battles with him over the question of staying on at school. This was an outburst at length with feeling about what is in fact a very complex relationship, and was listened to by the others in sympathetic silence. Then other girls told the group about their experiences. Everyone had 'played up' at school and everyone now regretted it. Mary, a lively tomboy very much spoilt by her father, told us how she had been in various troubles at school, had truanted to avoid punishment and how this had snowballed.

She then blamed 'them' – the school welfare officer, the education committee, the juvenile court and the probation officer, for giving her so many chances because she never really believed they'd do anything and now they had. As one of 'them' I led a brief explanation–discussion interlude along the lines that 'they' didn't like to take children away from home if it could be helped and must try to do the right thing even if by a process of trial and error. Some girls can accept the benevolent intentions of those in authority, others will pay lip service to them, but for a substantial minority in this and every delinquent group the idea is frankly incredible, and the whole purpose of our elaborate and expensive system for dealing with juvenile offenders is seen as to punish, or at least humiliate them.

At this stage, the hour being up, I closed the meeting. Georgina asked me why some girls had a psychiatric examination in the remand home. She is a babyish, lazy, intelligent girl whose hostility to the discipline of the hostel, and to me, had flamed swiftly and briefly on her arrival some weeks before to be replaced with a half-humorous resignation and comparatively non-delinquent behaviour. 'You know,' she had said with a grin at our first meeting after the storm, 'my mum's going to like you.' This sort of girl is better able to express an underlying general anxiety than the less intelligent and articulate member of the group, although it may be something they are nearly all feeling. It proved so on this occasion, because the others seized on this point at once.

Why were some examined, and others not? Why were they examined at all? Mary asked what would happen if they found out that you were mental. She herself always wondered if there was something wrong with her. I elicited that she meant psychosis and not mental deficiency, and then explained that this was a serious illness, unmistakable to any knowledgeable person, and that it was unlikely that we would have overlooked it in her case. On this I managed to end the meeting, Georgina lingering behind to say that she had never had a psychiatric examination and could her trouble be psychological? She'd been like this since she was six and she couldn't have been psychological then, could she? I laughed and said that we could start with that one next time.

There were two girls in this group who never spoke at all unless I addressed them directly, and then only with brief, noncommittal politeness. One, Cathie, was a withdrawn girl who never really opened up in group or individual sessions and the other, Jean, had come to us with a reputation for a violent temper and as having periodic fits of what was either hysteria or minor epilepsy. That night, soon after I had left the hostel, she had one of these attacks, screaming, running around, throwing the furniture about, etc. The staff and the other girls calmed her, she went to bed and slept peacefully and never in the months that followed had another fit or indeed showed any delinquent tendencies whatsoever, being instead particularly affectionate and helpful towards the staff and quite popular with the other girls. What that group experience meant to her one can only guess – I myself think that she saw her own ambivalent feelings towards her parents reflected in the other girls, with an effect terrifying at the time but reassuring in the long run; and that the reference to mental illness at the end of the session added to this reassurance.

Group work imposes a great strain on the probation officer. One is more exposed than in individual casework and in a delinquent group one is very likely to be exposed from time to time to extreme hostility. In this connection it should be remembered that hostility is revealed, not created, by the group situation, and the way the worker and the group deal with it can be a valuable and real experience for the hostile person which they would never have had if they had kept the relationship superficially civil.

Progress in group work will not fit into any neat pattern. For example, in my experience there is no steady progression either from superficial to deep matters or from hostility to trust. Groups have considerable mood swing and act out as well as verbalize. A communicative, emotionally charged session is quite frequently followed by one of stilted, carefully impersonal discussion tailing off before the hour is up – almost as if they felt that they had been seduced into relaxing their guard and resented it. Real happenings at work and in the hostel affect the mood of the group and these can sometimes be usefully discussed. In short, a chart of progress would read rather like a seismograph of earth tremors, as unconscious disturbances affect conscious communication.

The aims of group work, and much of the method, are identical with those of casework. That being so, what are the advantages in supplementing one with the other? Objective standards of success are unreal for both.

My experience is, however, that things do *happen* in groups more quickly and easily than they normally do in individual sessions. The worker gets to know people faster and more vividly – they are seen in the round, in a setting which simulates real life more closely than the one-to-one situation can. I think the clients see the worker in a more natural situation too and the relationship is strengthened by reality. In particular the isolated, backward, shy girl from a more or less antisocial environment sees her brighter and more self-confident companions enter into a relationship with the worker which seems to her at first incredibly foolish and dangerous, questioning, disagreeing, baiting, joking and so on. In fact she can see her own hostility acted out by someone else without calling down the retaliation she thinks inevitable. I have a feeling that a sort of composite picture of the worker is arrived at through the individual assessments – an Identikit picture which, while still not altogether accurate, is better than that which the more unstable and antisocial members of the group make if left to themselves.

In fact I seem to get closer to the client in a group and a little nearer to reality, and to do both these things faster than, as an experienced caseworker, I would have thought possible.

In 1938 Mary McCullough obtained a Certificate in Social Science at the London School of Economics. From 1939 to 1945 she was employed as a personnel officer. Since then she has been a Probation Officer and at present is working in the Middlesex area of the Greater London Council. She is co-author, with P. J. Ely, of Social Work with Groups, *Routledge and Kegan Paul, 1969.*

Further reading

AXLINE, VIRGINIA, *Dibs: In Search of Self*, Penguin Books (Pelican), 1971.

BARR, HUGH, *A Survey of Group Work in Probation*, HMSO, 1966.

BERRY, JULIET, *Social Work with Children*, Routledge & Kegan Paul, 1972.

CHARNLEY, JEAN, *The Art of Child Placement*, University of Minnesota Press, 1955.

FRAIBERG, SELMA, *The Magic Years*, Methuen, 1968.

KONOPKA, GISELA, *Therapeutic Group Work with Children*, University of Minnesota Press, 1949.

MCCULLOUGH, M. K. and ELY, P. J., *Social Work with Groups*, Routledge & Kegan Paul, 1969.

RICH, JOHN, *Interviewing Children and Adolescents*, Macmillan, 1968.

TIMMS, NOEL, 'Casework with Children' in *Casework in the Child Care Service*, 2nd edn, Butterworths, 1969, ch. 3.

WINNICOTT, CLARE, 'Communicating with children', *Child Care Quarterly Review*, vol. 18, no. 3, 1964; reprinted in *Disturbed Children*, ed. R. J. N. Tod, Longman, 1968.

WINNICOTT, CLARE, 'Face to face with children', Paper 3, in *Child Care and Social Work*, Codicote Press, 1964.

Index

Longman Papers on Social Work

Communicating with Children

Edited by Eileen Holgate

At some time or another, everyone is in contact with children.
Communicating with them should be easy, but it is not.
Adults somehow have a capacity to silence children. Although
parents and children may talk easily enough to each other, the
level of communication in ordinary families may be very shallow
and attention is sometimes drawn to this fact when a hitherto
amenable child becomes troublesome.

If this can happen in normal families, there are obviously
greater difficulties when relationships within the family are
faulty. For the child removed from his own familiar surroundings,
for whatever reason, the results can be very serious indeed.
Unless sensitive, understanding adults can tolerate his mixed
feelings and his unpredictable behaviour, the child may become
withdrawn or aggressive and unable to form satisfactory
relationships. This makes him appear difficult and uncooperative
when he is really hurt and unhappy.

This collection of papers covers problems experienced in
communicating with children. It is aimed particularly at social
workers and social work students who have a professional
responsibility for children. The contents include papers on
casework and groupwork with children in a variety of settings
and they offer proof that given time, patience and perseverence
there are ways of reaching children in critical situations, ways
of helping them communicate their inner feelings and ways of
preventing them from becoming socially and emotionally
crippled.

The book will also be of interest to other professional workers
with children, e.g. teachers and nurses, highlighting as it does
ways of enhancing relationships between child and adult.

Eileen Holgate, B.A., Dip.Ed., Certificate in Child Care, is a
lecturer in the Sociology Department of the University of
Liverpool, teaching on the Diploma in Applied Social Studies
Course. Previously she worked in the Liverpool Corporation
Children's Department, as, successively, Court Officer, Child
Care Officer, Area Child Care Officer, and Training Officer.

ISBN 0 582 42833 5

Longman